Fly fishing on wild becks

Secrets of the hidden stream

By

Pat Regan

Published 2012 by Can Write Will Write

http://www.canwritewillwrite.com

ISBN 978-148125-0009

Copyright © Pat Regan 2012

Pat Regan asserts the moral right to be identified as the author of this work

All rights reserved. No part of this publication may be reproduced, stored in a retrieval system, or transmitted in any form or by any means, electrical, mechanical, photocopying, recording or otherwise, without prior permission of the publisher.

This book is sold subject to the condition that it shall not, by trade or otherwise, be lent, resold, hired out or otherwise circulated without the publisher's prior consent in any form of binding or cover other than that in which it is published and without a similar condition being imposed on the subsequent purchaser.

About the Author

Pat Regan was born and raised in Southport, Lancashire. He is a professional author, environmental campaigner and dedicated, life-long angler. A countryman of various talents, Pat was previously a tree surgeon and later become a surgical chiropodist, reflexologist and sports massage therapist. He also helps his wife Cath manage a busy, preschool childcare facility.

Pat is the father of four children and he is also well-known in Ufology and Paranormal circles.

The author's previous books include:

UFO: The Search for Truth (2012, extended edition)

UK Paperback version:

http://www.amazon.co.uk/UFO-Search-Mr-Pat-Regan/dp/1479149128/ref=sr_1_2?s=books&ie=UTF8&qid=1345641012&sr=1-2

US Paperback version:

http://www.amazon.com/UFO-Search-Mr-Pat-Regan/dp/1479149128/ref=sr_1_3?s=books&ie=UTF8&qid=1345641227&sr=1-3&keywords=ufo+the+search+for+truth

http://canwritewillwrite.com/UFO.html

The New Pagan Handbook

http://thenewpaganhandbook.jigsy.com

Dirty Politics

http://dirtypolitics.jigsy.com

The Torch and the Spear

http://www.amazon.co.uk/Torch-Spear-Patrick-Regan/dp/1898307725

Peter Swift and the Secret of Genounia

US Version:

http://www.amazon.com/Peter-Swift-Secret-Genounia-1/dp/1478336595/ref=sr_1_2?s=books&ie=UTF8&qid=1345484821&sr=1-2&keywords=peter+swift+and+the+secret+of+genounia

UK version:

http://www.amazon.co.uk/Peter-Swift-Secret-Genounia-1/dp/1478336595/ref=sr_1_2?s=books&ie=UTF8&qid=1345484919&sr=1-2

Fly fishing on wild becks
Secrets of the hidden stream

By

Pat Regan

I dedicate this book to my great friend and supporter Tess Barnett

Preface

How does one get involved in what many reason to be a somewhat reclusive countryside sport, undertaken in extremely wild places usually with nothing more than a kingfisher or curlew for company? How does one gain proficiency in such elite circles, perhaps via books, magazines, lessons or possibly some 'other' way?

Hopefully the information that I shall impart within this book, gleaned from decades of practical execution on wild northern rivers, will assist the tyro or even inspire the adept towards a certain appreciation of the exclusive art of the dry fly fisher.

The dry fly is not a hobby, pastime or even a sport it is a 'religion' (or perhaps a cult) based on first hand contact with raw nature. Even when one cannot get down to the water's edge one's mental process is intimately projected there and personal thoughts are always on the weather and how it may be affecting the stream.

Dry fly is a love affair that improves each and every year. It is an untamed, pagan adoration of our organic link with what many want to comprehend but sadly never will! Words can never hope to truly explain this addictive mystery, which is born out of an ancient desire to stalk ultra wild quarry in equally uncultivated places.

Why stick with dry and ignore the wet fly? Well, for me the thrill of seeing a good trout, grayling or sea trout sip down a visible floating pattern from the surface film is the ultimate angling experience. Yes, I know that the wet fly or nymph (cast upstream or indeed down) will certainly on occasion take more fish but the numbers game is not in my opinion what it's all about.

Casting a dry imitation of a natural insect to rising fish is hunting in the purest sense of the word. For me it holds a persistent and electrifying fascination which never diminishes. One nice fish on the dry fly is superior to five on any subsurface method. This is angling paradise, though being confronted with vast rise forms on a gentle flowing run and having no dry flies at hand would surely be hell!

Furthermore it may be reasoned that one can be more selective and thus be more eco-friendly with dry as one can usually pick out the larger rise forms of adult fish and thus avoid hooking immature fish. The downstream wet fly cannot claim this virtue as very often that method relies heavily on catching fish that cannot actually be seen.

I genuinely believe that I owe much of my current passion for dry fly fishing to sun drenched days spent as a small child blissfully chasing sticklebacks, locally known as 'Jack Sharps', with trusty little net in hand around the flat moss lands near to Southport, Lancashire. The developing hunting instinct even extended to the noble pursuit of searching out frogs and toads in ditches, again on the Lancashire mosses and also near to the local seaside. All were always examined with a deep fascination for inhabitants of the aquatic realm and all where swiftly returned unharmed.

For me, these tiny rural brooks and ditches held a deep natural attraction as well as a frequently 'hard-to-catch' quarry which in its turn provided the basis for a learned 'wisdom', difficult to actually obtain by any other methods. This organic 'river-craft' gleaned as a boy now materialises as a great love for the countryside and most especially in a pursuit of our native game species, the brown trout and noble grayling.

I prefer to travel north to great rivers like the Hodder, Lune, Greta, Twiss and Doe. In such bleak locations one can discover truly wild fish, which can test the dry fly angler's ability and tackle to the full. The rugged becks of Yorkshire and Lancashire hold a certain enchantment for the brave souls who dare to meet them 'head on,' giving marvellous sport - second to none. Dry fly fishing on these beautiful rivers is often a somewhat neglected pastime which is a shame as it really is so very effective.

By studying this work it is sincerely hoped that the reader will come to realise the true potential of this extremely delightful technique.

Any angler who mistakenly believes that the dry fly is only for use on lush Southern chalk streams will with any luck gain an insight into the seemingly almost 'cult-like" world of 'Northern Dry' after reading this book. Furthermore, the fly patterns included have been created by the author, not for show but for good fish-catching effect after countless years spent observing the behaviour of the brown trout's diet and habits.

Let it be clearly understood; the dry fly is as deadly on the bleak, North Country Rivers as it is on the milder Southern streams.

If you do not believe this lofty claim then simply take the author to a beck of his choosing when the river and weather conditions are suitable. I will then be extremely happy to show you the ropes and introduce you to the 'cult" of the very much misunderstood Northern Dry.

Above: Author Pat Regan.

For as long as a man (or woman) casts a dry fly to a rising trout, the inquisitive child within will never expire!

Chapter 1

It's very nice if one lives in close proximity to a favourite watercourse yet life is of course not always that simple. Generally speaking, as a long-standing aficionado of the mysterious dry fly, most of my earlier trout hunting adventures has been undertaken as near to home as possible. Home is largely, as they say, where the heart is thus home for me in this instance is in Southport on the bracing North western coast of England, this meant that the grand old Lancashire Rivers and most especially the Hodder and Lune have been my private angling fixtures for over two decades; they satisfy every angling whim for me and are second to none.

  I do admit thought that at times I drift for a while into fly-fishing local still waters for trout, plus a day or two spent chasing sea trout and salmon when the rivers are bursting with spate water. Furthermore, a spot of local sea and coarse angling is also dabbled in on occasion, as and when time and commitments permit.

  We all need to move forward and my personal urge to travel, upstream like the returning salmon, finally got the better of me. Curiosity frequently gets its lethal talons into our quarry via a well presented fly and the very same enquiring wonderment often drives an angler upriver. I was no exception to this time-honoured, golden rule. Curiosity may kill the cat yet it also motivates the passionate angler to greater rewards. This very same wanderlust inquisitiveness drove me on to find out what came next after the Lune divided eastwards towards Burton-in -Lonsdale to become the River Greta. I just had to know directly what lay above Ingleton where the Greta itself branched off to become those beautiful Yorkshire limestone becks, the Rivers Twiss and Doe. What hidden secrets would I determine in the higher reaches of these lovely streams, where great waterfalls spilled into deep dark mysterious gorges cut brutally into ancient, lichen-encrusted caverns? I had read about such places but not as yet fished them.

I knew that these rivers were tremendously ancient places. The feeling of great age within was ever-present; it was so tangible that I felt that I could almost cut the heady atmosphere with my fishing rod! On one on the Greta's rock-strewn pools I had previously discovered some fossilised coral from the Ordovician/Permian era. This interesting find was millions of years old which really made me think about the enormous age of these upland streams. Silly yes I know but the site of a feeding stegosaurus would not seem that unexpected to the solitary angler visiting these locations. The imagination is given a new lease of life in such bleak and quiet river banks wherein the only company one is granted is from the local wildlife.

After numerous invigorating seasons of exploring these breathtaking waters I can share the following morsels with those fidgety souls who, like me, love roving after especially wild game fish in even wilder locations.

One's single most important ability is the capacity to be able to walk good distances when fishing these rough streams with a dry fly although it must be said the poor old feet do take a terrible pounding, especially on scorching summer afternoons when the sun-drenched rocks feel like they are trying to burn holes into the rubber of one's waders. Much of the fast, shallow pocket water, which may occasionally produce a brace to the wet fly, can at times admittedly be rather hard work on a dry. Nonetheless, fine sport can be had if you are fortunate enough to spot risers in these quicker runs; on the majority of occasions though I find that it's better to seek out the somewhat slower glides at the necks, run-offs and centres of deeper pools. The first ungainly footstep will though send spooky trout rushing for the safety of deeper water; ergo big fish often like to have the reassurance offered by these shady situations.

After spotting a rising trout, one needs to get into place to make the cast. Being a little down stream of your target fish is not always physically possible on rough streams as overhanging trees often dictate the way which you present the fly. When faced with an awkward trout that rises only about once every five minutes then I usually plonk myself down on the bank and, if it appears to be a big fish, wait it out. Constant intolerant casting at a finicky riser is both tiring and senseless. By prudently studying its rise forms, deciphering the diet which is causing it to be on the fin then waiting for that one 'right' moment, success is often at hand.

Above: The author fishing the River Lune in springtime.

If a hectic fly hatch is in progress then naturally you can afford to entice your riser with several well placed casts. If he is full of activity and avariciously feeding, then chances are if you are careful and don't throw the fly line over his neb that you won't spook him. This latter point is especially true when trout are tucking heavily into duns or spinners in rapid flows as in such places they are given little time to either take or reject one's feathery contribution due to the swiftness of the current.

With the great key of personal experience, one intimately becomes accustomed to knowing just where and when a pool will produce good sport. Water levels and general temperature too are crucial to success or failure. In summer, I find the best days are had on the Yorkshire becks when the sky is overcast with light to no wind, although a stiff breeze will at times stimulate hatches it has to be said. Excessively hot days simply drive the big 'uns into the deeper pools, although an adequately presented terrestrial dressing will occasionally tempt one out if he's resting under the shade of an old oak or willow.

As to water level, well to be honest these spate streams fish exceedingly well indeed, even when it's hot so long as there's a good head of water. I get particularly eager when I arrive at the water's edge to discover that the previous night's deluge has forced a couple of foot of floodwater into the beck. Disregard any thoughts of the luxuriant southern chalk streams; this is a different ball-game altogether!

Northern becks don't mess about – they quickly get rid of any surplus spate water, so before long the trout that have been lying out of the main torrent will be enthusiastic to get to grips with practically any imitation that dares to invalidate their field of view.

Fish can of course be highly discriminatory at the best of times on these becks; however, during the warmer months any half decent Blue Winged Olive (BWO) or rough olive dressing, tied on a number 14-20 light wire hook will usually be sufficient. To this lot add a selection of terrestrials, something to mimic the Pale Watery Dun on an 18-22 hook, sedges and an good assortment of spinner patterns for late afternoon and you're all ready to go at 'em - in the sharp end of business!

Occasionally a really choosy riser can be coaxed with a fancy grayling fly such as a witch or a red tag. Previous experience on the Hodder and Lune taught me that sea trout also appreciate a bit of red incorporated into my fly dressings. I have taken many good-sized 'silver bullets' even in extremely low water throughout the day with these two old-style imitations. A fresh-run 3lb sea trout on lightweight 6' midge rod with 2 lb leader is an awe-inspiring experience to relish for sure! Without doubt though, floods certainly give trout a hearty appetite as my best sessions have most always been had after these events on the Yorkshire/Lancashire becks.

When it comes to fishing under large waterfalls like Thornton Force above Ingleton, the angler can virtually adopt lake fishing tactics on occasion. Here the brown trout frequently cruise about in leisurely fashion, sipping hapless spinners and duns along the margins and away from the major impact of the main surge. Trout herein do not rush into anything – they largely take their time.

Thornton Force is around sixty odd feet high and the shock of all that crashing water coming over from the higher flat rocks is immense. You really do wonder if you should have brought your 'earplugs' when you get that close to the roar. Nevertheless, browns do feed in this awesome swell. Even when the water level is low in high summer the spray from this superb waterfall quite takes your breath away. It's as if the old Celtic gods of the place themselves were blowing natural liquid 'life energy' into your face and it is incredibly revitalizing indeed!

The whole place has a weird and wonderful quality of sheer power that is reflected in the beautifully marked sporting fish dwelling therein. Although viewing one's dry fly certainly isn't easy in such a choppy swell, the need to cast far is not absolutely vital to success. The main requisite is that your fly must float high and dry. If it doesn't then you simply don't see proper surface takes until it's just too late for your brain to register them and act accordingly. Therefore a good supply of Gink or other fly floatant is essential. You also need to be very sure-footed as it's quite easy to go head-over-heals (I speak from very 'wet' personal experience) and slip badly around these waterfalls. A signpost at the top of Thornton Force warns the more unwary walkers that there have been fatalities at this place. Depths can be very deceiving as well and what appears to be a safe position to cross the beck may suddenly drop into a dangerous watery abyss. You have been warned!

The wild fighting trout of these falls hit the fly exceptionally fast and you're often not granted a second chance to make contact so at all times keep your eye on the job at hand! Glance away for just one careless second and you misplace critical visual position of your fly, which ensures that important take you have been waiting for is missed.

As to what equipment to use; I find that I get more takes by using lightweight gear. My 6' 1" home-made midge rod with number 3 or (even No. 2) double-taper floater and 2-3lb 'double strength' tippet have served me extremely well for years. This faithful little outfit is great for quietly pitching a minuscule dry fly under overhanging branches or betwixt awkward rocks on the waterfall becks where longer rods are just a totally ham-fisted burden. The small rod becomes a marvellous extension of one's arm and before long you come to realise with its use that going back to the rigours of casting with a longer lake 'pole' is not a sensible option to take

Nothing is worse than trying to deftly flick a dry fly to a fast rising fish with one of those great big slow 9' so-called river trout rods! Why any serious angler should adopt such a cumbersome monstrosity for a limestone beck is beyond my comprehension! Perhaps it has more to do with machismo (mine's bigger than yours!) or the blatant expertise of the tackle advertisers art than the sporting desire to catch crafty fish on diminutive wild streams! Whatever the reason for the latter, alternatively the smaller rod is rapid, very accurate and soon becomes a fine friend to the travelling fisher.

Over the seasons, though I've had numerous trout over 2lb on the larger River Lune, my best Yorkshire beck brownie has been from the lovely River Twiss. I'd promised to take my young son Kyle up to this beck and on arrival we were greeted with hatches of both Medium Olives along with sparse showings of Blue Winged Olives (Ephemerella ignita). There was fortunately about a foot of slightly coloured water in the river which brought a smile to my face. On the third cast at a rising fish the fly was sucked under. Soon he was in the creel, a nice one for eating at just over a pound in weight. For a short spell, good trout seemed to rise all over the place. Anxious wagtails and dippers attacked each and every dun that drifted by while swallows and martens skilfully mounted spectacular aerial dives, like little blue dive bombers strafing an enemy procession!

We walked a few hundred yards upstream after landing two more trout. The afternoon wore on and sport calmed down to a snail's pace. A pleasant meandering run, treeless on my side yet well branched with overhanging alders on the opposite side, looked promising. Sure enough, I soon spotted what appeared to be a respectable fish rising quietly just behind a dangling bough some ten yards above me.

With my head bowed, I carefully flicked my pattern in front of his nose. I cursed hard as drag instantly set in. With the next attempt I snaked out extra loose line to combat the rippled current. The take came slow, not like one attempted by those feisty rough stream half-pounders. This was quite different and altogether heavier. Kyle had previously netted the other fish for me and was eager to have a go at this one too. However I refused his kind offer, knowing that I'd be bad company if he fluffed landing this bigger specimen. I couldn't put a great deal of pressure on the trout as I was, as usual, fishing with a light leader.

Beautiful golden flanks shot through with deep red spots appeared vital yards from my outstretched ABU flip-net. Nonetheless, on seeing this object the fish had other ideas and deftly shot out into the middle of the run once again. Several minutes later on an old gentleman appeared as if by magic behind us. "Looks like you've got a good one there lad!" he exclaimed. "Aye and it's taken some getting in" I replied, hastily glancing at the bloke whilst keeping my main concentration on the job at hand.

As I at last slid the fish into my waiting net, my little audience looked on in admiration. Everyone shared the moment. Two jam-packed pounds of wild Yorkshire trout lay glistening on the damp grass. In these days of intensively-reared Stillwater leviathans this may not seem such a big fish, yet on that dreamy halcyon afternoon in the warm August sunshine, it was a giant - fit for a king's supper!

The old gent was suitably impressed. "I've lived up 'ere over forty years and it's the largest trout out o' this water I've ever seen" he exclaimed in a gritty Yorkshire accent whilst walking inexplicably away as quickly as he had arrived off up the grassy riverbank. He was really quite a bit of a mystery! Who knows - perhaps he was an ancient angling spirit sent to bring us good fortune. We never found out who he actually was and we never saw him again. He disappeared into oblivion as quickly as he had arrived on the scene. Looking back over my previous angling records, its rather peculiar how often a lone stranger heralds a change of kismet when fishing. A hushed word is had with a solitary traveller then wallop! Your rod arches over as a fish struggles to get free. Funny old caper this fishing is for sure!

I caught six lovely fish that unforgettable afternoon and since then Kyle has also fallen for the watery addiction with several decent brownies (and grayling) taken on dry fly now under his belt. And what did dad have to make him for the following Yuletide? Yes, a nice little dry fly rod which is only 5' long. To be candid I'm rather envious of this sweet piece of equipment as is my good acquaintance Victor who kindly supplied the blanks. Its miniature dimensions will make it so handy for flicking a dun under overhanging branches. Come to think about it, Kyle will be able to reach trout where my 6' 1" midge rod will be, like those atrocious poker-like river rods, just too clumsy and large! Such is the irony of life – whenever I make something good for someone I always seem to end up wanting it back! Observant shrinks please make of this what you will!

The following dressings may inspire those courageous souls who wish to know what sorts of patterns do the trick on the often bleak limestone becks, the following special creations (invented by me) should be observed.

INGLETON DUN

Hook: 14-18 light wire
Silk: grey/olive, fine waxed
Tail: 3 whisks of grey cock
Body: grey silk
Wing: starling (split & advanced)
Hackle: (2) ginger and cream cock twisted through each other

THE DOE DUN

Hook: 16-18 fine wire, up eyed
Silk: olive
Tail: blue dun cock, 3 fibres
Body: fine black silk
Hackle: olive cock
Wing: starling split and advanced

WHITE & GINGER DRY YORKSHIRE SPIDER

Hook: 18-16 up eyed fine wire
Silk: olive waxed
Body: medium olive SLF dubbed
Hackle: ginger and white cock twisted through each other

    A secretary on a local Yorkshire angling club has been campaigning for some time now to restore the rivers Twiss and Doe to their rightful names. On modern maps one will see that the Doe is the 'Eastern' stream. This is incorrect and seems to be due to some mistake with the map compilers several years ago.
    The Doe is in reality the 'Western' stream which runs through Thornton Force with the Twiss being the Eastern beck running past the well-known White Scar Caves! Both of

these wonderful rivers hold big trout but the Western watercourse proves harder to fish because if is somewhat more inhospitable in its bleakness, making specimens rather difficult to approach in the higher reaches! The River Greta is quite a bit wider than the two smaller rivers above Ingleton.

In this book the rivers are sited by their 'original' names which are in distinction to the incorrect contemporary descriptions. It is imperative to bear this point in mind to prevent any confusion.

Chapter 2

I was exasperated with myself for not rolling out of bed earlier. Yesterday the heavens had opened which, by any stretch of the imagination, appeared to make a triumphant day's limestone beck trouting very slender indeed to say the least. Paradoxically, today the grey clouds had parted sufficient blue sky to patch a fisherman's jacket and the gorgeous Yorkshire streams would soon be dropping to a delectable shade of port wine red. My prime objective was the River Greta below Ingleton, the stunning little tributary of the famous River Lune. Today my instinct told me that the larger Greta would be transporting enough surplus flood water to make the sixty five mile trip from my home in Southport well worth the exertion.

Although the River Greta gets a late run of salmon and sea trout it was only the wily native browns that drew my attention. Higher upstream above Ingleton, the river divides into the Doe and Twiss which are both exceptional becks in themselves for flicking a tiny dry fly at natural, free-rising trout.

On arrival at the water's edge I was not disappointed. The preceding afternoon's downpour had brought the river up to between one and two feet above summer level which was now fining off to a good-looking fishing height.

Several noticeably excited grey and pied wagtails joined together with swifts, swallows and energetic sand martins in an impressive airborne display surmounted against the glut of local insect life frequenting the chaotic surface film. It was a dry fly angler's dream come true.

As I carefully forded the brook to reach an enhanced tree-lined pool the concentrated aroma of moist, wild garlic and luxurious white hawthorn bloom greeted my nostrils. A melodic pink chaffinch set his uneasy gaze on me from an old, overhanging willow branch as I crept gently up to the water's edge, eyes and ears intimately searching for valuable rise forms.

A nice semi-smooth run, occupied by what appeared to be a first-rate constantly rising fish, held a good pace now which was usually absent from this particular flow when water levels proved a little lower. In dried up summer days without the required previous downpours this petite pool stagnated into an especially unhurried glide, which held nothing but the scantiest curiosity for any cheerful dry fly fanatic worth his salt.

Fish, and big fish at that, would often be seen slothfully rising in this torpid, canal-like stretch of the Greta with a conceited self-assurance gleaned from their awareness that they were all but indestructible from the attentions of the angler. I remember one particular evening when my eldest old son Kyle, who was only ten years old at the time, was almost driven to insanity whilst attempting to lure these red-spotted teasers. With proficiency and purpose of will he tried his very best to get these sneaky and highly educated trout to oblige. I had warned him that he was wasting his energy yet the passionate doggedness of early youth clogged-up his hearing better than any ear plug from a chemist's shop could ever have done.

Little boys and large cunning trout rising to flies on smooth calms are an unstable combination. Consequently, in no time at all Kyle developed a relatively psychopathic detestation which was tempered with a kind of cynical, drudging reverence for the maddening leviathans inhabiting this awkward pool.

However, with the water levels up though, today was a different thing altogether. I felt my heart miss a beat in anticipation as I located myself near the run. The wind was subsiding nicely and the aerially pitching swallows gave proof that duns were hatching off the surface in abundance. Spurwings, Medium Olives, various gnats and the odd untimely Blue Winged Olive appeared to be holding the curiosity of the fish. There was though an additional fly, somewhat larger than an Iron Blue Dun yet just as dark. Even though at first hard to identify against the peat-stained tinge of the surface, I quickly caught a specimen for recognition in my hand. As I correctly assumed, it was a Purple Dun, (Paraleptophlebia Cincta).

On an earlier trip to the Greta I had noticed a few Purple Duns farther down the stream. At the time I made a rapid mental note to dress up a few of these miniature beauties on my fly tying vice when I got home. Of course, I ought to have managed to find time for this possibly significant task yet owing to other pressing activities my dressing session was omitted. Accordingly, only two satisfactory, but as yet unproven, Purple Dun imitations were fashioned and given home in my fly box. This was a detail that I would presently come to dearly regret.

The majority of the trout in this pool were showing under the far bank almost fifteen yards away. I wasn't positive either as to just what they were taking, although by the evidence of existing rise-forms it was a fair-sized insect that was now holding their focus.

Very cautiously, with head held low I cast a Purple Dun out to the initial and closest temptation. With intermediate velocity and no feasible drag, the sample drifted silently over its objective without any effect.

Lifting the line off the water, I gently shot the diminutive fly out once again. The take came as if in slow motion and with an encouraging vigour that really got my adrenaline overflowing. A definite flick of the wrist and my first trout of the afternoon suddenly took line at a speed of knots like these large untamed Yorkshire fish regularly do. Several exhilarating moments later I unclipped my little net to land the fish which was now almost mine. As I arched down to draw the trout toward me now quite breathless the unimaginable happened; with a closing effort and splash he threw my fly back at me and was off, back to his watery realm.

Whilst cursing my bad luck; I examined the number 16 dressing. I'd been playing what I'd estimated to be a fine wild fish of approximately two pounds not realising that the hook was broken. I didn't for the life of me recollect thrashing any boulders with the back cast, yet there was the proof of defeat in my hand - a pattern entirely cracked off at the bend. This is thankfully a rare occurrence but it does seem to happen at the most inopportune of times.

Not to be put off, onto the leader went my other Purple Dun. Lunch was really being dished up now as by this time several good sized browns had started to mop up flies drifting all over this pool.

The next fish I hooked weighed in at just under a pound was properly landed and returned to grow into a big 'un! I then lost an additional two trout, which I could only put down to misfortune as they both dropped off like the first disappointment had done right at the net. A few more trout rose to my Purple Dun but came exasperatingly short of actually taking the offering. Ten minutes drifted by devoid of too much fuss then another flotilla of different olives produced yet more frantic activity on the surface. Things were getting exciting!

This time it was rather different though as around approximately twenty trout rose intensely, thrashing the surface like whirling dervishes. Two more first-class wild trout were then landed on the Purple Dun that fought very well and tipped the scales at a pound each. Inquisitiveness was now starting to get the better of me and I found myself wondering if these aquatic Yorkshire inhabitants would take any of my old beloved dry patterns or were they really just lining up exclusively for this innovative Purple Dun design?

Over the next half an hour I sacrificed my fishing time by trying out quite a few of my typically efficient, all-purpose standby flies. Ginger Duns, Blue Duns, Medium Olive variants, and a plethora of other home-spun fluffy wonders were carefully presented to the fish without so much as a polite peck in return.

With frustration starting to set in back on went the Purple Dun and bingo - I was immediately into battle yet again. Today at least, the trout only wanted this purple pattern alone – no other would do! They attacked it with the same type of secure fervour noticed by the angler when stocked rainbow trout are excitedly harrying terrified coarse fish fry. This is in my experience moderately rare as the old universal dressings mentioned above will nine times out of ten get some kind of reaction from the Yorkshire fish. Even when trout are being blatantly discriminatory my 'generals' can habitually be relied on to produce some interest. The Purple Dun on this day however was crowned the 'Sovereign of the Greta' and no other watery aspirant to the throne would be adequate!

Undoubtedly I could have landed many more of fish from that pool but again inquisitiveness and itchy feet got the better of me. Would additional or even possibly bigger trout be also rising in the swifter pools downstream? I constantly have to ascertain the answer to this everlasting and yet challenging question.

Personally, I believe that rambling up and down the river is a fundamental part of the gratification of fly fishing. The prospect of seeing a lovely green woodpecker, kingfisher or the darker gloominess or paler luminosity transgressing a pool not perhaps as tree-lined as the last one - a chance sighting of a mysterious otter or apprehensive roe deer drinking from an oaken pool - natural things such as these oblige the curious, hunting spirit to search out the secrecy of whatever lies 'just' around that next meandering bend in the river.

The committed dry fly angler has largely to become an amateur naturalist if he/she is to be as successful (and happy) in his/her sport as he truly desires. As the afternoon wore on, weariness came upon me like a dark velvet shroud. It was becoming increasingly hard to not in fact sit down on the rock-strew bank and fall fast asleep. Trekking over eight hot miles in my thigh waders, I'd caught quite a few wild trout over the one pound mark and had now begun to make my way back indolently to the first pool that had given me so much previous exhilaration. Silver shafted light patterns from the warm summer sun gave the slow pool an almost metallic luminosity. Delicate swaying willows created ever-changing, runic shadows on the virtually translucent water flows. All felt well and proper in the world! Even though I had only been away from this place for an hour or two it felt good to be back and yes, the fish were fortunately still on the fin moving well now too, although not in their former magnitude.

Upstream I went to the head of the pool and without any indecision I soon snaked out a good line with the Purple Dun to the nearest candidate. "Idiot," I cursed at myself as I ineptly missed the rise by being too slow. Exhaustion, with its inborn lack of attentiveness, is the worse adversary of the dry fly fanatic.

I knew that common sense was evidently dictating that I should at least sit down and close my eyes for a while, but the well-proportioned fish moving close to my location forced me into making a final resolute endeavour to secure this prize.

I remember very well one unquestionably successful old Lancashire salmon angler of my acquaintance named Jerry, who could habitually use his inherent magnetism to lure the silver bars out of the River Hodder, in the vicinity of Clitheroe, when less significant mortals had packed up their gear and headed for the car.

"When the fish are there, you have to just fish for 'um," Jerry would often say to me in his no-nonsense, yet affable Lancashire fashion. Jerry's great secret was childishly uncomplicated. "If you don't keep ya line in the water then ya won't get any fish onto the bank," he would call out with a somewhat comical paternal astuteness that was gleaned from a lifetime studying his quarry.

The old man's almost 'childish' angling philosophy stayed with me on numerous difficult occasions when the chips were down and led to big catches on difficult days when most rods had given up and headed for the comforts of home.

Oddly, Jerry's laid-back, yet exceptionally perceptive words of heron-like tenacity rang clearly in my ears right now although I'd not seen the chap for some years as unhappily he'd gone off to that immense stream in the sky following a brief illness.

Trying to shake the increasing drowsiness from my head, I launched out a longer line to a riser that had resisted my earlier efforts and this time I made contact. Milliseconds later a red- spotted beauty was taking line from my reel at high-speed, dashing for the security of the other bank. Applying profuse amounts of side strain I managed to impede the action from getting too unstable for if this fish had made it to the distant side then there would have been danger for sure, as sunken willow branches and the roots of alders were in ample supply therein.

Although I was delighted at my belated achievement I abruptly realised that I was not now by myself. A modest assembly of elderly ramblers had taken up residence behind my spot on the pathway next to the river's edge and were eagerly jostling through the undergrowth to get a better look at this complimentary countryside entertainment.

Of course not wishing to disillusion these smiling and happily waving woodland spectators, I decided to try and make the 'entertainment' seem rather easier than it really was for as my prey leapt away once again I haughtily played it while seeking to place my rear end down on a hefty rock which I assumed was only about a yard behind where I was standing. Regrettably however this particular rock was farther away than I'd originally anticipated as I discovered to my cost, stumbling clumsily and nearly filling my thigh waders with extremely cold stream water.

Now feeling more like a pantomime celebrity than an experienced dry fly angler, I eventually managed to save face and reached the safety of the large rock. "Fool" I mentally kicked myself while throwing a somewhat artificial smirk in the general direction of the clearly pleased onlookers. However, all was not lost as the fish was still on the line and actually now feeling as worn-out as I was. A well-mannered string of colloquial "Ohs!" and "Ahs" with a few polite hand claps for good measure from my newly- established fan club greeted me as I climbed out of the pool, finally triumphant with a chubby trout of about one and a quarter pounds securely in my net. I through them a gracious gesture, grateful to reach dry land in one piece and off they wandered contentedly up the pebbly footpath. Those nice old folk didn't quite appreciate just how close to losing this fish their reluctant comedian had really come by trying to be such a cocky so and so! All the same, the pleasure of that particular circumstance was symbiotic; without question the fond recollection of that comically pastoral moment in time will for numerous years live in the in the minds of all parties involved. I find that the Yorkshire folk are such agreeable people by and large!

This little walking party had in one respect brought me good fortune with this late-in-the-day fish. Nevertheless, the gods of fate soon had the last snigger as my only enduring Purple Dun finally fell desperately in love with the top branch of a large shrub, which has regularly been known to have an almost magnetic draw for one's best fly dressings. Subsequent to this minor disaster, I tried out some of my standard olive imitations and then some of my never-fail terrestrial dressings. I even resorted to the odd colourful grayling and tiny midge jobs but something deep within told me that the magic of the day had now ended! I was quite satisfied with the spectacular sport I'd had that day, for nothing greater than the sacrifice of my pair of killer patterns, under the welcome shade of the lovely summer willow trees.

The trout had now gone off the boil and I, somewhat unwillingly, packed up my six foot rod and set off for the long journey down the motorway to so-called civilisation. The Purple Dun had worked its first extraordinary charms on the attractive wild inhabitants of the peat-stained Greta.

THE PURPLE DUN

Hook: 14-18, fine wire
Thread: fine grey waxed
Tail: fancy ginger/white cock
Body: purple SLF (dubbed) or purple body silk

Rib: black thread
Wing: stub of dark grouse wing rolled & tied upright
Hackle: ginger cock with a hint of white

The Purple Dun can be tied in smaller sizes (16-20) to replicate iron blues. However, a darker hackle may be better for this purpose.

Chapter 3

Fishing inspiring waterfalls, especially big ones such as Thornton Force (or Fosse as it used to be known) and Snow Falls close to Ingleton, Yorkshire, can undeniably be a very invigorating experience. The same can also be said for the quieter stretches of river that cut through the Yorkshire Dales. Magical spots where no man ever seems to ramble and the only substantial life forms one is likely to encounter either sport horns and say "moo" or possess rough white, woolly fleeces matted with spiteful prickly thistles and dock. I dearly love these places for in them one can get nearer to the genuine essence of nature, and thus closer to oneself!

You'll be sadly disillusioned if you're expecting to find any fifteen pound stock fish, synthetically reared in some high-tech genetic stew pond in these fine-looking areas, yet to me personally a one pound wild brown is worth a multitude of the former. It's all relative and herein size is most defiantly 'not' what matters the most!

Angling is, for some of us at any rate all about getting back to our aboriginal organic roots. It's about being in desolate lonely places in which the only thing between you and raw 'tooth and claw nature' is your intrinsic intuition for self-preservation. I do not make this assertion frivolously, for the seemingly temperate Yorkshire becks can be treacherous subsequent to a brief downpour, turning good dry footholds into glassy slides straight into lethal hidden depths. An agreeable day's angling very soon transforms into a life or death nightmare when one's head unexpectedly disappears underneath the rapids. This I personally know, not from any 'third hand' experience, but from quite a few hands on close calls which still remain in the mind as a significant warning.

By no means ever wade into unfamiliar depths however secure they may initially seem and never try to overextend your distance on these waters just to get that bit extra into a cast for life is too precious and it just isn't worth the underlying risk involved even if you're a trained lifeguard!

The great dangers of all waters, particularly those with a secret undercurrent, have always held a deadly charm for man. Our primordial Celtic ancestors even saw fit to exemplify this energy force in the semblance of the mythical Kelpie whose folklore is particularly popular in the Scottish Isles. This fierce water-sprite took on many forms the most frequent being a big black horse or a tall, angry woman garbed in green who would tempt the unsuspecting to their watery doom in the nearest deep pool.

The Kelpie was also believed to give warning of impending storms by wailing banefully, which would carry on through the tempest. This relationship with thunder was thought to rise from the sound of its thrashing tail as it submerges under the water. Kelpies also had a positive side though and were thought to occasionally assist millers by keeping the mill-wheel running in the evening.

Any person who's ever fished a flood-engorged salmon river and observed the sinister, swirling brown currents and the massive amount of organic materials washing past will have a certain understanding for this old indigenous legend. Conversely, past experience has led me to believe that the local tradition surrounding the Kelpie may have greater links to our indispensable survival instincts than we may at first care to appreciate.

Could perhaps the Celtic folk in their wisdom have presented us herein with an essential extrasensory defence message ingeniously put in place, not to scare us as usually seems to be the case with many old ghost tales, but to actually help fishermen and hunter-gatherers far from their dwellings to stay alive?

The Celts of course had a profound spiritual empathy with the land, seeing spirits and gods in the hillside, trees and streams. They were an exceptionally poetical and nature-orientated society that used many shrewd analogies to get important messages across. Precarious places also gained their serious consideration leading to mythological explanation for good reason as we see herein.

Some years ago I recollect, while night fishing for sea trout on the River Hodder seeing something that still makes me wonder. I was having a few last casts with a silver and green lure across a deep pool which had, half an hour before, given me a lovely energetic three pounder. I'd decided that it was time to finish off and head for the car park when I saw, what appeared to be a woman ever so silently walking up the pool. She was not on the rock-strewn bank but in fact drifting 'over' the river itself just about fifteen yards away from my spot. It was in the region of two thirty in the morning. The night was very dark with no moon or shadows and before long the unearthly apparition simply disappeared into the gurgling black watercourse, accompanied by the evocative cries of an owl high in the surrounding alders.

I left the river, not afraid, but in a state of tranquil amazement feeling vibrantly alive, a sensation which still remains with me to this day! Perhaps this 'Grey Lady of the Stream' was really a beneficent danger sign sent from the old Celtic gods that inexplicably protected this wild little tributary.

This peculiar vision didn't seem logical as such an aquatic achievement was physically not possible. The run was in excess of ten feet deep in the middle and it held a fatal flow. I shook my head and rubbed my eyes as I thought I must be either dreaming or hallucinating and I certainly wasn't inebriated.

In retrospect, I in fact did feel quite indebted, rather than scared, that such a strange spectre joined me on that warm summer night. Who knows, if she hadn't then possibly I wouldn't be here today unfolding this strange account! Nevertheless, kelpies, undercurrents or whatever you want to call them are all interrelated on different planes of reality and danger remains to be danger any way one interprets it. It's never too far from the appealing yet treacherous surface film so do take the safe alternative and be vigilant for if you don't then you may be keeping the kelpies closer company very much sooner then you would ever wish to.

Regrettably, the fundamental survival feature within our nature which eventually connects us (on many levels) to the real world and protects us has been in principal suppressed and almost bred out of us by the synthetic, ultra-modern culture in which we now inhabit.

Even on the most packed out reservoir, the angler who may have little or no curiosity in wild rivers still feels the inbred desire to break free and find him(her) self some private breathing space. Therefore, a small deserted bay on the hectic lake brings with it a momentary sensation of deliverance from the socially -wagging tongues of the clambering masses, which always demand polite response.

One thing is certain, the deep need for emancipation from our fellow human beings and the ceaseless quest for natural seclusion materialises in all sorts of different ways. Perhaps unusual pastimes like float tube fishing are now so trendy principally because they present anglers with an opportunity for much needed isolation, via drifting away from the idle chit-chat of the bank side crowds! So who really cares if you are doing an extremely good impersonation of a big duck with a hat on, as long as peace and quiet is achieved?

Sportsmen now appear to be setting off further a field to find seclusion. The world is increasingly accessible, at least for those who can have the necessary funds. For some of us though, solitude can be had not only on the cheap but very much closer to home. It isn't compulsory to venture out to the uttermost corners of the earth to find extraordinary wild fly fishing activity. The unpretentious rock-strewn becks and waterfalls of Yorkshire, Cumbria and Lancashire hold vigorous, red-speckled riches for the rare minority that accept the challenge to discover their concealed mysteries.

To get a flavour of this exhilarating drug one only needs to visit the region neighbouring Ingleton in Yorkshire for here you will discover more solitude than you could ever envisage. The landscape is ruggedly stunning and the dry fly fishing quite splendid. Without doubt trout can regularly be had on wet fly or small nymph pattern too but I basically prefer the explosive action guaranteed when a finicky brownie hits the drifting surface imitation.

Virtually all the standard dry river patterns for imitating fully developed flies are effective at their specified time although I, like many other investigational dressers, have copious amounts of home-spun flies that I hold dear for the Yorkshire streams. To mention but a few, the ginger and white-hacked Thornton Olive and another good specialist dry fly of my design, the Greta Dun, are never too far from hand as they have proved their merit on countless occasions.

That most impressive cascade Thornton Force, which I mentioned above, is in excess of sixty feet in height and the brown trout that inhabit this particular spot are understood to be part of a waterfall-locked, original genus. This is because the fish in this pool cannot, for apparent reasons, go upstream and over the vast fall; neither can they travel far 'downstream' past a nice place called Hollybush Spout, for if they did then their chances of safe return would be nigh on zero. Moreover, local anglers have mentioned to me that this pool may be sporadically topped up with fingerlings from above Thornton Force if they can only survive the shock of the sixty plus foot plunge. These tough browns are then some of the wildest one can catch and must breed somewhere between the two waterfalls mentioned. Catching them on the dry fly is great sport with the white foaming spray coming off the waterfall full in your face.

The furthest side of the Thornton Force pool seems at times to be the most prolific spot to rise a fish. To be truthful though, at times persistence is necessary as they will not always oblige herein and can also be fairly hard to please as to just which parts of the pool they choose to feed in. The ruse is to cast your fly as faraway as you can over to the rocks then take up any slack by softly retrieving line until you get the fly back to your position. You will find that the normal choppy swell created by the waterfall will push your dressing back to your position but it's important to keep in contact as takes are exceptionally fast and you'll miss nine out of ten chances if you're too sluggish with your strike.

I believe that early on in the season or later in the day are the best times to fish this pool as it can get quite fashionable with ramblers and other sightseers when the sun decides to peek out. Even though the trout may be especially wild in this pool it defeats the purpose of gaining vital seclusion if you extend your welcome and just become another preoccupied thing of family entertainment for a crowd of joyful, rucksack-carrying walkers. Not that there is anything at all wrong with folk getting out and having a good ramble into the countryside – far from it, if more families bothered to seek such pursuits instead of spending their summer evenings glued to the television soaps that we would perhaps all live happier lives.

Travelling upstream over the trail to the river above Thornton Force you will discover the upper River Doe. Alas, most road maps are incorrect here and give this beck as being the River Twiss. By the way I believe that some angling clubs are seeking to get this confusion sorted out and have the names corrected back to their original geographical locality. Human beings are uncommon creatures on the Doe and it can be a deliciously austere and bracing place at times because of the noticeable absence of tree cover, yet the Doe does certainly hold its own kind of strange fascination. It's a stunning high limestone stream in the most traditional sense and the trout herein are of an excellent size. They can be tough to approach though in low water conditions, yet again thanks to lack of foliage cover, so do keep your head low so that you don't scare them!

Subsequent to a good deluge of excess water from the lesser becks things can change radically with inhibited easily alarmed trout coming on the fin and rising with self-assurance in the sherry-coloured flows. At that time, a good afternoon's sport can be had with a regular variety of imitative rough olives, terrestrials, spinners and the odd sedge dressing for good measure as the day wears on. As always, my loyal six foot midge rod with a double-taper, number three (or even number two), floating line always accompanies me on this brook to good effect.

When one finds that the Doe is too low for good sport then it's time to head back down to the River Greta, below Ingleton. I adore this beck which is not unlike the upper Lune, the main river into which the Greta flows. This primordial river can be fruitful in all conditions even when moderately low yet, as with the Doe, a nice downpour will always revive the place and encourage fly hatches.

Often, a single hard-come-by fish means more than several on an easier day. One trout that I landed on this beck was especially hard won as the water levels were, much to my disillusionment, exceedingly low. The sun had been hammering down unremittingly on my head and I was beginning to feel that I was wasting my time. However, as the brightness of the afternoon light began to grow fainter, I noticed a few risers in a swift run under an elderly dry stone wall. These crafty fish were tucked in firmly against the fern-covered projection and although not hard to cover they were quite awkward to present the fly to because of frustrating currents which led to that old enemy of the fly fisher - drag. Managing to punch out a loose line, I mended it a little upstream and on the fourth endeavour a fish hit my dressing with a hearty splash. It wasn't a gigantic brownie, about one pound at a push, but it made quite a few rod-bending athletic leaps to recover its liberty after mistaking my Greta Dun for a late meal. Consequently I believe that I could have stayed on and caught a few more fish however though I was tired, I was contented on that occasion with just one fish.

Now and then fly hatches prove to be paltry affairs and the water levels may be low. At such times the angler must either go home or probe deep into his capital of previous experience if a fish is to be grassed. Yet, when the sand martins are swooping so skilfully into the fragile swarms of spinners dancing inches above the water's surface and the peat-stained stream fines down into a pale red after a heavy flood, there cannot be a more exhilarating place to be in the world than the Yorkshire becks for the passionate dry fly fisherman.

These special places hold a sacred charm that can only be fully appreciated via the type of intimate and solitary relationship found between the lone angler and untamed nature. Without doubt, the challenges are always different, never the same, with every visit presented by the wonderful Yorkshire becks and waterfalls each new season.

THE GRETA DUN

Hook: 18-14, fine wire
Silk: orange or red, waxed
Tail: blue dun cock
Body: grey goose herl
Rib: fine gold wire
Wing: red grouse primary slips tied split and advanced
Hackle: natural red or dark ginger cock hackle

THE THORNTON OLIVE

Hook: 18-14, fine wire
Silk: grey waxed
Tail: natural red cock
Body: pale dubbed hare's ear (well picked out around the thorax)
Rib: fine gold wire
Wing: coot or moorhen primary (rolled and tied upright)
Hackle: fancy, ginger and white barred cock hackle

Chapter 4

Every so often the enthusiastic fly tier stumbles across a somewhat different dressing or method of his accidental yet happy creation which really proves a hit with one's prey. The following account relates but one such small instance!

Successfully catching classy browns on the rugged streams of Yorkshire is for the most part dependant on favourable water levels. I'd been restlessly watching the river heights as weekend approached. Extreme floods usually squash all hope of a good day's fly fishing as do periods of intense, weed-laden drought, however, because of the nice drop of rain that had only just fallen, tomorrow would most likely be ideal.

Perhaps I am the exception to the rule but these days, instead of sensibly tying my flies well in advance of an angling trip, I recurrently knock up a few hasty dressings the night before I leave for the river. Consequently, true to form, on the evening before my intended mission into the rough country with only one hour or so to spare at the fly vice, I started to envelop the bare shank on a hook with thin thread.

I wanted to fashion a universal olive artificial which was intrinsically difference, thus after a few attempts and with a fair degree of reverse thinking the 'Retro Dun" first saw the light of day.

So what was the subtle difference between this prototype and the rest of those winged beauties sleeping peacefully in my fly box? Simple!

The Retro Dun, as its name suggests, is dressed 'backwards.' Instead of tying the wings in the usual dry fly position I'd placed them at the tail end, inclined back past the bend of the hook. The hackle was then added before a short body as the thread made its way back to the safety of the head position. Looking at the finished fly, I felt convinced that it would be helpful in hatches of various olives such as Blue Winged Olives, Pale Wateries etc owing to its natural unobtrusive appearance.

The materials for this new-fangled fly were quite meagre yet easily obtained. Ginger and white barred cock hackle, coot primary for the wings and as for the body material, well its surprising what one can achieve with one or two snips of your teenage daughter's brownish tresses. Fiona was glad to oblige yet we had a slight difference of opinion about the actual colour of her locks. I claimed it was "mousy brown" Fiona said "no way" it wasn't, however I had to admit defeat after examination of the hair dye products in a local chemist shop. 'Ash brown' is then the 'authorised' body colour of the Retro Dun although I still prefer to call it "mousy" - that is when Fiona, who incidentally used to be a keen martial artist, isn't in the immediate vicinity!

Driving past the impressive River Lune close to Hornby, Lancashire, my son Kyle and I noticed that the water level was about two feet higher than the normal summer height. The waters would be dropping off nicely later this afternoon as we approached our selected objective, the striking River Twiss above Ingleton, Yorkshire. We left the vehicle in a little car park some half a mile past the famed White Scar Caves entrance on the B6255 to Hawes. Subsequent to one or two swift egg sandwiches and crisps we eagerly put the rods up. Except for a couple of extremely weary potholers, who plonked down by their vehicles and drew deeply on their apparently much longed-for cigarettes, we saw practically no one else in the car park.

There were though two affable German tourists who graciously smiled and enquired "Will you be going fishing?" Bearing in mind that we were scrambling like rabbits down a stony wall, clad in thigh waders, carrying rods and heading in the immediate direction of the adjacent trout river the question seemed somewhat irrelevant. Nonetheless, although Kyle farcically whispered to me "Tell 'em we're going to play golf dad!" I did the respectable thing grinned back politely and replied "Oh yes, what a pleasant day for it!" They smiled back watching us go our way!

We trekked off down the muddy field towards the silvery little beck, taking our leave of so-called civilisation and our curious new friends. Luckily, the substantial herd of sometimes over-inquisitive brown cattle that frequented this area were at the far end of the pasture. While they had never actually attacked us, a couple of the more playful bulls had moved rather too close for comfort once or twice in the past causing us to walk that bit faster. Most over-welcoming cattle go away when one taps them resolutely between the horns with a fishing rod but these large, and at times territorial, Yorkshire lads are a quite different thing altogether.

Upon reaching the waterside I anxiously tied on a Retro Dun. The river was in fine condition and before long we spotted several steady risers in a little twisting pool with good pace. On only the third flick of my six foot midge rod a decent brownie rose and arrogantly nailed the fly. "Hey, this Retro thingamajig really works well" I exclaimed to Kyle, who was flabbergasted at the speed in which the new dressing had performed its duty. Trudging swiftly over to my position, Kyle immediately snapped out his landing net to assist me. If ever there was a natural born gillie it was Kyle. This youngster never misses with his net and actually prefers to land fish for others rather than catch them himself.

I didn't fancy carting fish around in the heat on the midday sun yet, so we carefully returned this trout which weighed one pound. A couple of minutes later I caught another decent wild fish again on the increasingly successful Retro Dun. Several more fell to this pattern before we decided to drive over to the River Doe, another lovely limestone beck three miles away. I dare say we could have stayed and caught fish all afternoon on the Twiss but the wanderlust got hold of us. Moreover, I wanted to see if the Retro would also take fish on another stream.

The Doe is a much more windswept stream, having little in the way of surrounding tree foliage. It does however have a rough hewn beauty all of its own and a few deep pools with large fish. Often all one hears on the Doe is the sad cry of a lone curlew or the jingly-jangle call of a high skylark in the wild blue yonder. Sometimes it's so eerily quiet here that silence rules supreme. It really can be quite extraordinary with no sounds at all; no cars, birds etc and when the wind drops it is very weird indeed.

As I had expected, the Retro did the business equally as well on this watercourse and produced seven athletic fish. Sadly, none were monsters yet all fought like wild aquatic tigers. Furthermore, I now had a deadly new-fangled dressing which had produced the goods on two different streams and was impatient to try it on other waters.

Several weeks after this highly enjoyable Yorkshire trip I was given the opportunity to introduce my 'killer fly' to the fish of the River Hodder, near Chipping in Lancashire. My old pal Vic had called around to my house on the Saturday afternoon to give me a hand with a job in the garden. The weather was fairing up nicely after some previous very heavy downpours so Vic suggested that we take a trip to the Hodder the following day.

The next afternoon was almost a text book late summer's day for dry fly on a Northern spate stream. It was quite warm, robins were clicking away in the high alder trees and the river was a fantastic shade of pale sherry brown. Hopes were high for some good sport to come.

After hurriedly eating a couple of paste buns I motioned to Vic that I was going to have a go at a constantly rising fish some twenty yards above our picnic spot with the new pattern. A few casts later I was carefully playing a fit grayling that used its big sail-like dorsal fin to full effect. So even the 'Silver Ladies of the Stream' ' approved of my Retro Dun.

Next, a nice fat brown trout attacked the Retro with gusto. Before long Vic joined me and was soon into another grayling, albeit on a pattern of his own making. We fortunately appeared to be smack bang into the middle of a shoal of hungry grayling with a few trout for company. Vic also lost a possible sea trout in a small deep run under some overhanging alders. Over the seasons, I've personally had quite a number of sea trout on dry fly in broad daylight, fish that have clearly enjoyed being guest to the resident grayling shoals. Maybe the sea trout feel a kind of secure affinity with fish like grayling that also possess silver bodies.

That afternoon was quite magical. There was a sort of heady seasonal transformation in the air which all creatures, including us, were beginning to feel. Even a lone bat was experiencing the intoxicating conditions of this late summer's day as it silently fluttered in and out of the dancing clouds of olives, seemingly oblivious that it was hunting in warm full sunshine. Most of my fish took the Retro Dun tied on a size 16 hook; two that didn't fell for a 'Grayling witch,' an old-time favourite of mine for the Hodder.

These two 'fussy' grayling were proving very hard to please as there was a plethora of assorted insect life coming down onto the surface for them to snack on. "Right," I said to myself. "If you don't want the Retro then munch on this Witch!" My quick change produced a good grayling straight away. Later, with

Vic standing close by, another fish which was being choosy prompted me to try the 'Retro for Witch' changeover tactic once again.

"Hey Vic watch this, I'll have this one on the next flick!" I bragged with a grin. Comically and much to our surprise the change instantly worked and this awkward riser hit the Witch like a ballistic missile. We both laughed but, as most experienced grayling fishers will tell you, this often forgiving species is frequently partial to such quick change techniques. Persistently casting an 'unattractive' fly to the grayling will sooner or later just put the whole shoal down. Although I spent quite a large amount of the time on this particular day trying to snap photographs, we landed about twenty fish between us which were mostly grayling the best of which weighed one pound. We kept two grayling plus one trout for cooking, the rest were returned to grow bigger.

On the way back along the farm track to the car we spotted a tasty added bonus. What at first looked like a large skull in the grass turned out to be a large Giant puffball. These strange fungi are highly prized by chefs and this was quite a big one.

Vic suggested that we should tell the local press back home about our odd find. They were actually very keen to come and photograph it and the following day my family had the pleasure of a most unusual gourmet treat. Anyone who's never eaten fresh grayling with giant puffball, lightly fried in butter, has never lived! Talk about delicious!-It's certainly a feast fit for a King!

The Retro Dun was the real star of the day yet again. It had marked some memorable adventures and provided wonderful dry fly sport in two counties second to none.

THE RETRO DUN

Hook: size 18-14 fine wire
Thread: fine grey or olive
Wing: Coot or Waterhen tied split, (to lie over and past the bend of the hook, like a tail in effect)
Hackle: fancy ginger and white barred cock, (tied in front of the wing at tail end)
Body: several strands of 'ash brown/mousy' hair (off an 'agreeable' girl) then varnished for strength

GRAYLING WITCH, (REGAN'S VERSION.)

Hook: 20-14 fine wire
Thread: fine black
Tail: red wool
Rib: fine black thread
Body: dubbed black wool
Hackle: palmered cream or white cock hackle (applied full length of body)

The Retro Dun can be effective at any time of year and will take fish during most olive hatches when dressed in various sizes. A size 16 is possibly the most useful pattern as this is about the right proportion for imitating the BWO, LDO and other more commonly encountered river olives.

The Grayling Witch is an old fancy pattern that will also take trout and sea trout when conditions are right. Although it is a fancy pattern I believe that it actually imitates many leaf hoppers and other colourful terrestrials which fall into the water. It is especially effective after windy conditions and when the leaves are starting to blow onto the water.

Above: The Author dressing a dry fly.

Chapter 5

A lot may be written about grayling but much of the available literature may unfortunately be based on older misconceptions and third – hand knowledge. The following comments are, like 99% of my observations, taken from true life experience.

Clear mental pictures frequently come flooding to mind when we discover a box full of old, tarnished angling photographs and I recently found myself drawn back into such a warm realm of fond memories when I stumbled across a forgotten consignment of snaps that I'd taken some years ago on Lancashire's lovely River Hodder, near the town of Longridge.

Soon after the salmon fisher has put away his tackle for yet another long winter, rivers such as the Hodder and Ribble come into their own good form for a small but devoted minority of anglers who realise the great sporting prospective of that 'Silver Lady of the Stream" - better known as the mysterious grayling, Thymallus thymallus!

Much of the wonderful imagery of this mysterious and lonely old spate stream is for me largely recollected in rich foliar shades of gold-tinted browns, deep basic olives and autumnal yellow with vivid orange hues competing with the peat-stained port wine colour of the receding deluge.

My special and long-lasting love affair with the Silver Lady stretches back numerous seasons and has at times been somewhat more like a 'love hate' relationship with this elusive species. This is however in the main self-inflicted because of my single- minded, and yes I admit 'stubborn', dedication to the dry fly method.

In those earlier days I would, like many others, be quite happy to peacefully fish my little time-honoured 'team of three spiders' through the cold mountain rides and tumbles of the November stream. Even the weighted nymph or upstream wet would present the exhilarating requisite 'buzz' at that unpredictable moment of silver-flanked contact! Nevertheless, life isn't always simple and before long the terribly compulsive dry fly addiction caused me to abandon the longer customary river rod for a miniature home-made, six foot weapon armed with a lightweight number three double taper fly line on a small reel and a loyal assortment of home-made dries dressed down to as minute as size 24 hooks. Ah yes, once, before the dreadful dry fly obsession took complete control of my otherwise even-handed senses, I would regularly catch nice bags of grayling on a well presented wet fly such as a Red spider Waterhen bloa, Snipe and yellow or any other delicately fluctuating river wet dressing.

I must point out here that there is nothing wrong with fishing the subsurface fly and it can be an extremely exciting technique in the correct hands. The wet northern spider patterns are also a joy to tie so long as they are made properly by dressing them short on the shank and with sparsely applied hackles. Many examples which you will find on display in the tackle shops are less than useless for in the water they hold little resemblance to the drowned duns and hatching nymphs which they are supposed to represent. However, I put the rationale for my own progression towards dry fly down to deeper levels of hunting instinct. Unquestionably, the nymph and wet fly fisher will on the odd occasion catch more than the dry fly angler. This is not in any dispute, yet the elation of that luscious 'visible' surface take is to me personally worth any three subsurface plucks from greedy trout.

My previous mention of hunting instinct relates to that basic feeling of in some way 'knowing' the best place and time to expect good rises to transpire! This extraordinary 'knowledge' is only gleaned through time, via lengthy riverside experience and is not something that can be purchased for cash or effortlessly learnt in an airless classroom. The seemingly insignificant natural sights and sounds so important to success with the dry are often missed by the long casting wet-fly fisher. This is not to say that there's anything wrong with the latter, it's just that for me personally, the excitement of finding that rewarding surface take is altogether unsurpassable!

Meandering gradually upstream with a purposeful gaze and looking for that remote little whirl in the surface film; discerning the slight audible variation between water hitting rocks, falling autumn debris or a good-sized grayling leisurely gulping down a late olive dun. Expertly observing that almost imperceptible movement in the current that gives away the position of a good fish gently taking drowning spinners; over the years all these mysterious events and countless more sharpen the hunting angler's instincts to a state of excellence with a dry fly! Herein resides the kingdom of the silent, stealthy yet highly attentive mind – the naturalistic hunter and the tracker who has no patience to wait for the fish to come to him.

To be quite frank though and at risk of displeasing some old hands, there is at times something inconsistent with the protocol adopted by a lot of inconsiderate river wet-fly fishers. On many occasions I have seen such anglers absolutely wreck lovely rises by romping straight into the swim and practically standing on the head of a good shoal of feeding fish, proceeding next to rip a long destructive line downstream without thought of the ramifications. Unsurprisingly, this imprudent conduct has usually sent every self-respecting fish into a gigantic panic and resulted in them rushing out of the main stream for the nearest safety of cover. This unsporting behaviour of course isn't entertaining for the poor old dry fly fellow who has to wait for perhaps an hour before the river and its startled residents recover their earlier self-confidence and start to rise once again!

River craft is what it's all about (or at least should be) however, unhappily this vital old rural lore appears to be a bit sparse these days in a lot of places. It never hurts to respect the other chap's right to a fish to two and spoiling his chances through clumsy conduct on the water in simply bad form all around!

In many ways I believe that anglers are now being ingeniously indoctrinated by influential manufacturer's marketing campaigns into believing that without their lightweight and high-tech equipment it just isn't worth taking yourself fishing! You can go out and spend thousands of pounds on the most excellent gear but without the long-acquired instinctive hunting skills required, successes will be very hard won indeed! I feel then that excessive prominence is granted to flashy paraphernalia and unreasonably expensive reels, rods, lines et cetera; items that do more to line the manufacturers' pocket than the fly fisher's creel!

A splendid well-varnished seven hundred quid boron rod just doesn't seem such a good buy when a cunning neighbourhood farm boy outperforms its self-righteous owner with his granddad's scruffy old glass- fibre or bamboo trusty casting pole!

I recall that the renowned Jack Hargreaves of the Thames T.V. Countryside/Out-Of-Town programmes was my definitive idol as a school boy. I would rush home to watch those fascinating shows as fast as I could. His wonderfully unsophisticated rural attitude must never be forgotten for it contains an ancient indigenous angling acumen which we are in jeopardy of losing forever! Newcomers to the countryside would do well to study any material they can access on old Jack for therein resides true rustic wisdom.

Our primitive ancestors when out hunting in the field relied heavily on their intrinsic instincts for survival and so must we too. Substituting them for a dependence on contemporary technology is an error that we must safeguard against at all costs and perhaps the most significant point when stalking game fish on the wild spate streams is to be 'responsive' to your immediate situation! Use your eyes, ears, senses of smell and remain on alert at all times not only for success in angling but also for the sake of your own personal security. A lethargic mental attitude in the countryside leads to danger for oneself and no fish in the bag.

Unless you are fortunate enough to find an obliging shoal of ravenous risers eager to forgive your obstinate attentions, thrashing away at the water is both monotonous and generally fruitless. Grayling can be tolerant of such things at times but not always.

Grayling of the wild becks are in fact at their best from about late July onwards depending on the weather. Though, on sweltering humid evenings, when the odd sea trout splatter about teasingly in deeper pools, the 'Silver Lady' can be especially hard to entice to one's fly. And if you're getting a bit weary and exhausted then it makes good sense to withdraw from the water and have a rest until you feel your energy return.

The tiny white so-called 'Fisherman's Curse', or Caenis and other diverse minute insects are often the reason for grayling being hard to tempt. These flies are seen in their millions at times on hot afternoons and the fish really do enjoy them. However, one generally needs to fish with very diminutive patterns to replicate this insect down to size 24 hooks. If you have been previously fishing with say a size 16 olive or gnat then chances are that when the fish switch to caenis feeding they will totally ignore your larger flies.

For the duration of these lively periods your size 16 hook can look like a shark hook. The best response I find is to scale right down to No. 22-24, fine wire hooks. You'll also need to trim your leader down to say around double strength, 1 lb. breaking strain or comparable line for if you don't then you'll most likely suffer wretchedly from stacks of annoying prods, pecks and missed chances without that much required final contact. Moreover, trying hard to cast too far is both frequently needless and excessively strenuous when fishing the 'Curse Hatch' for grayling or trout. The best course of action is to search for regular risers near enough to permit you to essentially observe your fly. This tiny fly and light leader 'close-line' system of approach applies equally when fishing practically any other tiny imitation as well.

Yes, a swift change from a larger dun imitation to the tiny pattern can pay dividends and before long the takes will start to come in fast. A hushed rivulet seemingly before devoid of all life, albeit the occasional dipper, can suddenly renovate into an excess of vigorous fish when the curse arrives on the water in good numbers. These flies get in your cloths and in your face and hair but they can and do make for excellent fishing if you have the correct dressing to hand at the time.

Long casting when using ultra fine double strength line at these times frequently leads to bust tippets, so do hunt out the closer rise forms and leave any far-off contenders until their diet alters afterwards. High-speed striking is not always a great idea either and may result in missed fish simply because the grayling are at these times quite preoccupied with nailing as many natural flies as they possibly can before the banquet is over. One must be well focused, determined and target individual risers most accurately rather than just casting willy nilly into the general shoal and present the tiny dressing with adroit attention and great care.

Now and again, caenis-fixated grayling will fall for a well-presented larger fancy type dressing like the Grayling Witch, Red tag or Treacle parkin. By the way, grayling can be extremely voracious on occasion with hefty specimens occasionally being taken on huge sea trout affairs such as muddlers, tube flies and medicine-type flies in the wee small hours of a summer's night! As with other species, grayling appear to become more predatory in their diet when they get older. Somewhat erroneously we often call treacle parkin etc 'fancy' patterns, nevertheless there is an overabundance of hoppers, wasps and beetles which sport vivid red, yellow and orange tints in their makeup. Actually then with our use of such so-called fancies we are inadvertently imitating certain natural insects, that find themselves caught up in the stream, even if we fail to actually appreciate what kind of bug it is at that specified moment in time!

The old fancies usually come into their own when the stream temperature plummets later in the season subsequent to a pleasant summer day or in the chilly winter months when drabber flies are in shorter supply.

An additional dressing that I would be reluctant to exclude from my fly box at any time of year is the Pale Watery. Grayling in particular are exceptionally partial to this petite fly and it's frequently a big mistake to omit this pattern from the water when fish are taking small unidentified flies at distance. It does need to be tied with a modicum of care and a certain amount of representative accuracy though as fish can be hesitant to take scruffier examples of this fly at times – I know this from personal experience.

The stunning River Eamont near Penrith, Cumbria is an excellent stream too for grayling and they are fond of the Pale Watery on warm late summer evenings. I recall once visiting the region in late August with a companion for the trout fishing and amazingly we hadn't even realised that the watercourse held a good head of lusty grayling.

One experience on this beck springs to mind. I remember that I was stooping low behind an overhanging willow when I saw what appeared at first to be a small group of trout, contentedly rising to a good hatch of flies, which were unaware of my presence. I hastily tied on a dry Pale Watery to match the hatch in progress and on the third cast I connected with something that felt rather solid.

Before too long I gained line on the subsurface monster which had been pulling like a train. A enormous dorsal fin at last broke through the dark waters arching my little midge rod over into a vicious curve.

My pal who had by now come over to see what the commotion was all about had to agree that they were strange looking trout in this river as he clapped his eyes on the silver-flanked grayling thrashing about in the water. A few thrilling minutes later, we landed the gorgeous, pear-eyed 2 lb grayling and gently slipped it back to fight another day.

We were both especially delighted to find out that grayling actually existed in this watercourse. Why we had never even considered this species to be present is still a mystery to us but present they were and we felt most appreciative to have found out this fact via first hand experience.

Afterwards, just as the final silvery webs of that memorable late summer day light glanced off the river, the fish had a brief mad bout of surface activity. This concise evening rise didn't last very long yet I managed to grass another stunning 2 lb silver lady from a tricky run in between the long pulsating outcrops of emerald green weed growth. This was fortunate as tying on flies was now almost impossible due to the failing light and thoughtlessly I had not thought to bring a torch along. Apart from these two excellent and unexpected specimens I caught just one lonely brown trout from a tree-lined farm pool which would have delighted any true dry fly angler worth his salt!

Yes, we can all wax lyrical on the romantic golden summer evenings like this spent by the waterside – they really ought to last forever yet, like the rich fly hatches we seek, they never do! The universe is constantly expanding and new experiences are always around the corner, ergo we must move forward to greet them with new hope. River Hodder grayling can grow as large if not larger than the silver ladies of Cumbria

The big Hodder specimens sometimes appear without warning. One day you will find only undersized fish, then a day or two later the big 'uns of over two pounds each turn up with remarkable assembly of ravenous giants rising to flies in the very same swim! I wouldn't surprise me if a record fish was produced by the Hodder one day.

Hunting this species in winter on the spate streams is indeed a joy. Why wait for the rising trout of spring when the Silver Lady of the Stream is so cooperative in the icy, bleaker winter months? If you possibly can, get there a few days after a respectable deluge succeeds a dry spell. The additional turbulence of 'a bit of fresh' will almost guarantee that good heads of grayling start to come on the feed as the waters fine off into attractive sherry hues.

Can there be any better angling gratification than to catch such truly wild fish as the grayling when other mortals are at home, dreading the impending dark heart of winter's wrath? In the dark months there's nothing to match the feeling of arriving at a nice calm grayling run in October with the raucous call of a cock pheasant breaking the chilly morning air; Jack Frost's freezing veneer on the white-laced spider webs and hazel branches or the slight drifting aroma of burnt stubble in the meadows and that exhilarating first riser moving progressively beneath a mature overhanging alder.

Yes, to the minority of resilient souls who defy the odds and venture onward into this dynamic climate the rewards are extremely great indeed!

Effective grayling patterns for the northern spate streams are as follows:

THE FIRE BUG (GRAYLING FANCY)

Hook: 16-20, fine wire
Silk: fine white
Tag: bright red and yellow floss or wool followed by one twist of gold lurex
Body: peacock herl
Hackle: natural red cock

REGAN'S PALE WATERY

Hook: 16-22, fine wire
Silk: fine white or grey
Tail: blue dun cock
Body: grey goose herl
Rib: yellow thread
Wing: Waterhen or Coot wing slips (split and advanced)
Hackle: pale blue dun cock

TINY WHITE CURSE BUSTER
(Use in caenis, midge or tiny reed smut hatches)

Hook: 20-32
Silk: micro fine white
Body: white S.L.F or fine wool dubbed
Thorax: black mole or rabbit fur dubbed
Wing: white poly-yarn or wool (tied spent as with spinner patterns)

Chapter 6

The triumphs or failures of the passionate dry fly angler, who firmly refuses to hang up his gear just because there's hoarfrost on the ground, are also dependant on the existing restrictions forced on him by the state of the day at hand. Even so, there's seldom a month, week or day that cannot give an hour or two's dry fly sport with grayling or trout providing that the angler possesses the principal requirements for success which are vigorous zeal, craftiness and a single-minded will to win through at all costs.

Normally speaking, grayling spawn from March to May although of course the climatic conditions play a significant part in this seasonal matter. Moreover, if one has right of entry to a watercourse which holds the Silver Lady of the Stream then there's no reason to exclude this exceptional species from your angling list. If you do, in favour of being 'TROUT ONLY', you will unhappily miss out on some fine sport and also the chance of an exceptionally delicious gastronomic delight as well. I believe that a one pound grayling, scaled and cleaned out then grilled with a touch of black pepper and butter is every bit as excellent on the table as brown trout. In some ways they taste more like sea fish and the flesh is paler than most trout too. Furthermore, as they are a 'free-rising' shoaling species one can frequently bring home enough for a hungry family meal when they are in a suitable mood to take one's flies. Never though take more than you require.

The River Hodder, near Clitheroe in Lancashire has provided me with some of my best catches of this fish. Furthermore, I found through personal hard won practice that the murky days of January and February recurrently produced the heaviest grayling. One uninviting yet ultimately exhilarating February day which I recall with great fondness some years ago on the Hodder saw the watercourse falling gradually but still running quite high and slightly coloured after the heavy winter floods.

Though I wasn't expecting any great angling success at this chilly phase in the calendar, at least the river wasn't iced up like it had been on my previous visit. Winter on the Hodder is not to be taken lightly. On that earlier trip, the only way that I would have caught any fish would have been to use a 2-piece hand auger; drill holes in the solid ice and dangle a baited hook like the natives apparently do in Alaska and other frosty regions.

When it freezes keen on unsympathetic, yet stunning, northern spate streams such as the Hodder it does so with impressive style with ice then thick enough to walk on making an angler feel quite redundant as the fish stare indifferently back at him through Mother Nature's cold, glassy casement. Nonetheless, now it was February and the immense frosts were mercifully losing their grip on the river earlier than I'd expected.

Before long I noticed the bright lemon flicker of a curious grey wagtail, quickly popping out across the stream from her moss-covered bolder which caught my eye as I warily strode across the bank side gravel. This omnipresent little riverside dweller was apparently hunting the odd olives from the surface film then eagerly devouring them on her well-placed, water's edge vantage position.

After observing this natural treat for a few moments my understanding of an otherwise despondent looking day changed dramatically. Hatching duns of course meant the opportunity of surface feeding fish and I personally knew from prior experience that this particular stretch frequently held a good head of powerful silver ladies.

Because it was winter there wasn't much leaf on the surrounding trees. However, I still had to be watchful with my back cast for behind my position a high and near vertical fossilised rock face with overhanging branches endangered every flick of my lightweight fly line.

The pool I was on had a nice steady run at the tail and, sure enough, a few little grey sailboats were beginning to litter the surface film. It was midday and, much to my delight, some large Dark Olives (Baetis rhodani) were apparently putting in an extremely welcome early appearance.

It's the fly that gets the fish off the gravel and looking up toward the surface, consequently it's the redeemer of many a dry fly aficionado's day. I personally adore this modest insect for it has the capability to get the adrenal glands flowing on all but the bleakest of days, often popping up in the beck when no other fly dares to venture out into the open waters. Amazingly though, many anglers turn up at the stream and seem quite unconscious to the hatching LDO, or any other surface fly for that matter. For me, the LDO is continually representative of the promise of summer.

Unhappily, many fishermen prefer to thump out a heavy nymph or wet fly across, or even worse, downstream to discover their sport. If I had a pound coin for each time I'd seen careless anglers wade right in and totally spoil a lovely hatch of olives I'd be very wealthy by now.

My heart starts to sink if I arrive at the stream to see an outline in the middle of the river waving about one of those great beach caster-like rods downstream. When this occurs, I usually amble off in the reverse direction and give the stretch time to recuperate. Such statements as the above are outwardly prejudiced to many wet fly enthusiasts, yet they are formulated from countless seasons of vigilant surveillance of the behavioural patterns of my quarry. As soon as a fish sees that shadow of a downstream line coming across its vision in low water conditions it usually dives for the deepest cover possible - just like a terrified bunny down a bolt hole. This isn't merely a personally held belief or any type of angling snobbery; it's a straightforwardly attestable 'fact' that can be witnessed by any person who cares to study the matter.

Many times on the northerly waterways I have caught fine quality game fish right in the shallows (six inch deep or less) at bank side whilst irritated mid-stream wading addicts have gone home with unfilled baskets.

Myself, and a friend who shares my apparently 'cultist' attitude of stealthy hunting on these grand little streams, regularly used to jest that the 'downstream only' wet fishers were incurably afflicted with some sort of untreatable angling malady. Years later, I now think that we were mistaken to joke because it is indeed a quandary that many anglers seem powerless (or reluctant) to abandon from their psychological process.

Subsequent to ten minutes of searching the water for a decent rising target, an unexpected large swirl behind a grey semi-submerged rock grabbed my interest. I didn't visually witness the fish but judging from the swell it was a fine specimen. Without restraint, my dry LDO artificial dropped nimbly just to the side of the rising fish, which was less than five yards out from my casting position.

Once more a heavy swirl was seen, a deft flick of the wrist and then – 'slosh!' He took it brutally first cast. Although I felt his mass for a millisecond, I was too damn slow and failed to hook him properly. I quickly false-cast through the air to dry out the pattern and my heart missed a beat as the large fish rose with assurance to third effort.

Again I struck and instantly reprimanded myself as I abruptly realised that this grayling had not taken my reproduction but a genuine insect drifting only inches from my fly.

Discretion now seemed like the best alternative so not wanting to scare this fish I retrieved my fly and exchanged it for a somewhat different pattern, which was generously treated to a fresh rub of tacky floatant. Already, three or perhaps four other risers were starting to take notice in the local insect carte du jour. My concentration was however intimately focused on the one particular fish which I knew was of very decent quality.

The pattern I had on was one of my old personally devised favourites, the Blue & Olive Dun. I fashioned this particular fly in the 1980s with the LDOs of the River Lune in mind but hadn't had much occasion to put it through its paces on the Hodder at that point in time. While I am usually a paid up sponsor for the 'winged' dry fly fellowship this pattern and a few others like it are the exception to my 'self enforced' regulation.

The Blue & Olive's immense appeal lies in the method in which the twin hackles are twisted through one another. This quite simple procedure creates a good natural sparkle to one's fly which the fish recurrently cannot refuse to accept. A few of my angling friends, that share my love of the dry fly, have also had success with this straightforwardly learnt technique. So good was this dressing that I wrote about it quite comprehensively during the 1990s in the angling press.

This unassuming imitation has a sturdy yet classical appearance which seems to defy the straightforwardness of its construction. Consequently, when dressed well its sturdiness is second to none. More importantly, the fish really do take it well particularly when the LDO puts in a welcome emergence.

It's also quite lethal when the Olive Upright, (Rhithrogena semicolorata), is on the water later on in the season, usually just in time to welcome the Morris Dancers skipping around the May Pole. What a great fly this is! It's exceptionally unproblematic for anglers to classify, looking like a somewhat large LDO, and game fish will frequently drag it down sadistically like fit lions ambushing elderly zebras!

Unlike our wild trout, the grayling has a reputation for clemency toward the angler and this can be especially true when the fisherman is faced with a big ravenous shoal of medium-sized grayling. However, larger specimens are at times annoyingly tricky to entice. Unsurprisingly, the bigger fish are that size mainly because of their intrinsic capability to keep out of trouble with us anglers.

Hefty grayling will often rise once or twice then merely disappear from sight for hours or even days much to the irritation of the postulant specimen hunting angler.

Nevertheless, I was apparently faced today with a small number of good quality fish that were indeed in a tolerant frame of mind.

As the dark armada of duns increased in number on the surface film, I cast out the dressing once again. The short-lived rest period must have done the fish some good for my fly instantaneously disappeared under the chilly, dark brown, foam-covered stream. Once again I tightened into the fish which, this time, felt well connected to my line.

My focus was momentarily disturbed by the fabulous metallic blue and orange glint of a speeding Kingfisher very close by which threatened to take my attention off the job at hand as it almost flew into the arc of my fly line.

Usually I adore to see these gorgeous little river birds but today this one was really pushing his good fortune. Undeterred, I kept an unyielding hold on my fish as it made a gritty effort to seek the protection of the far bank. It was now running very hard, deep and almost taking my line onto the reel backing when it unexpectedly stopped stone dead. Putting any amount of pressure on this specimen was right out of the question as I was using only lightweight, 'double strength' line of only 2.12 lb, B/S.

For what seems like eons, the fish just lay there, glued to the bottom of the babbling stream in a deep ravine some twenty yards away from my position.

I hadn't yet set an eye on my expected prize and was starting to in fact wonder if I'd actually hooked a small salmon, a sea trout or even a large chub as can often happen on these streams by mistake. Yes, the latter are frequently encountered when using light gear on these northern streams and all can be real demons to land, taking sometimes upwards of an hour to get into the net. Contrary to accepted belief such events, whilst being without a doubt exhilarating affairs, are an unwanted annoyance when one's sights are firmly fixed on hunting classy grayling. However, my original instincts were accurate and it was a grayling on the end on my line.

Before long the specimen surfaced, displaying that greatly pleasing and highly characteristic dorsal fin which glistened like a sparking roman candle on Bonfire Night as it caught the late afternoon bronzed rays of the February sun. Minutes later my outstretched flip net found its pear-eyed mark, as I cheerfully heaved the sleek beauty from the wintry waters.

This particular Silver Lady weighed in at 'two and a half pounds;' an admirable specimen grayling on any tributary and very satisfying on a cold afternoon.

As the day wore on quite a few smaller grayling and an out of season sea trout of about two pounds fell to my little pattern. It was getting pretty chilly now and although I'd enjoyed some fine sport, I toyed with the thought of getting back to the car for a nice hot drink from my flask. As I cautiously trudged over a great damp bounder, watching my step, I was abruptly startled by the vision of an additional human being. Such creatures are exceptionally uncommon on these rough northern streams, particularly on the lonesome Hodder at this austere time of year. Actually one is more liable to see an elegant, yet retiring, stag than another humanoid out here in the native English backwoods.

Nonetheless, this small person was no stranger to me. A sardonic smile issued from the young man as he approached me. "Hiya there Pat, have yer caught out yet?" Andy the local farm boy was always anxious to know what was being caught in the stream. His broad Lancashire brogue was welcoming as he stumbled on the treacherous wet rocks up towards my position. Andy frequently used to appear, as if by magic, on days otherwise vacant of human contact. From time to time he would be armed with his old, solid glass spinning rod in the expectation of landing a gigantic Hodder salmon or sea trout.

I have to admit that I never actually observed the lad catch anything with that tuna-class monstrosity yet I had personally witnessed a fish of over thirty pounds caught in this particular pool several years before. However, today Andy was not fishing but apparently probing the stream bed for other fishermen's' snagged up spinning lures which would occasionally get lodged on the jagged, near to surface, boulders of the watercourse. This shrewd little collection hobby had a two-fold advantage. Not only did it offer a good 'gratis' source of spoons, plugs and Devon minnows it also cleaned out the river of environmentally hazardous items lost on earlier high floods. As far as the losers of the tackle were concerned their shiny spinners were gone forever never to be seen again yet it was 'finder's keepers' and Andy was a dab hand at this hobby.

I must confess, I found a few lures myself as well on occasion. Conversely, this activity was not without its intrinsic dangers as more than once in the past I foolishly managed to overstretch, when attempting to salvage a stuck lure that was almost within my grasp and gained an unrehearsed drenching for my troubles! Going completely underneath the river's surface on a winter's day certainly cannot be recommended either, although all the noise of the stream's flow becomes a strangely peaceful hum when one goes right under. It's not surprising how swiftly one learns from such asinine mistakes and how quickly lessons like this are absorbed into the consciousness. Such is the nature of the survival instinct.

Andy and I sat on a rock and I informed the lad about the nice fish I'd taken before he came down that afternoon. He asked me to hook another large grayling 'to order' as he wanted to see how hard they scrapped. Even though he'd observed me land a lot in the past which were smaller he'd never seen one so huge as a two pounder.

"Okay you're on, I'll show you how it's done!" I boasted to Andy with a wry wink, not in actuality expecting to ever match my previous efforts. "Give us yer net and I'll ' land it far yer if yer get one," offered Andy politely.

While Andy's personal experience on this earth had given him natural country astuteness far beyond his tender eleven years, his fish landing skills were to say the least fairly controversial. His heart was certainly in the right place, yet his technique of landing anything that travelled through the river was rather peculiar.

Not wanting to be too unkind or unappreciative it had to be understood that the lad's technique could be compared to a blend somewhere between an incredibly infuriated bee doing battle with an inaccurate net-flinging gladiator, trying too hard to please the baying rabble in a Roman arena.

Above: Hodder Grayling caught on dry fly.

    Many alarmed angling souls had tried to explain this difficulty to Andy before but at the critical instant youthful enthusiasm would always take over and in he would leap, arms thrashing wildly about at the hapless fish like a being possessed. Such splashy debacles habitually resulted in the angler's prize regaining its liberty, so I courteously refused Andy's well-meant offer and kept the net securely latched to my fly vest.
    As I glanced up at the heavens I noticed that the light was soon to depart as dirty mustard-coloured snow clouds gathered ominously on the western skyline. I had no plans for being caught out here on the Hodder in the pitch darkness at this time of year so I mentally promised myself

that no more than quarter of an hour was all I was permitted before going back up the steep hillside towards the little car park.

The earlier brisk falls of LDOs had vanished, or at least I thought they had, and not a single fish broke the quite surface film. It was now very hushed on the blackening stream.

I was just about to turn around and pack up when a sudden heavy splatter in the beck some five yards out caught my attention. With fervour once again renewed at this unexpected occurrence, I called over to Andy. "Hey, did you hear that one? Looks like an excellent fish!" I rapidly flicked my little pattern out into the current and before he could reply my reel was yet again singing a merry tune with the double taper number three line rushing through the rod rings at breakneck pace.

The frosty breeze of the February afternoon was quickly forgotten as the fish leapt out of the dark mysterious river like a ballistic missile with an unseen target. Andy breathlessly romped, half stumbling on the sharp grey rocks over to my location. "Hey that's a good 'en Pat" he yelled, hardly able to restrain his excitement. After several nerve-jarring minutes the large silver grayling drifted peacefully into my awaiting landing net on its flank.

I was silently thankful that I'd respectfully prohibited Andy from practising his fish landing modus operandi on this particularly nice specimen! If I'd given the lad the benefit of the doubt and let him have a go with the net he may have messed up and lost it for me. The chances are that would have resulted in Andy following the 'missing trophy' into the river via me chucking him in frustration! Well alright, maybe not, but I would have been more than a little bit 'disgruntled' to say the least for quite sometime to come nonetheless! This lovely fish was a double for my earlier prize and it subsequently tipped my spring balance at the same extremely pleasing two pound mark.

"There we are pal, that's how you do it!" I exclaimed with a smug grin as Andy looked on in youthful appreciation.

"You wanted to see a big grayling on the bank so here it is!" I continued. Being a fairly practical country lad, he of course didn't wish to appear 'too' impressed. "Just Jammy I reckons, nowt but jammy" he said dryly as I laughed out loudly in reply. Andy was clearly quite flabbergasted at this fish and obviously extremely bowled over to see such a lovely silver specimen, which he'd previously ordered, right there before his eyes on the bank.

The raucous cry of an old cock pheasant broke the cold air in the icy stubble field above the river as Andy and I climbed back up through the woods toward the muddy farmyard car park. The smell of cows and the filthy pasture surrounding the farmstead hung in the air like rich, organic soup and it was simply marvellous.

"See yer next time Pat." Andy threw me a friendly wave as he heaved himself over the rickety wooden gate towards the warmth and safety of his hilltop farmhouse. I responded light-heartedly as I watched him head for home. "Goodbye now Andy - next time we'll get some 'bigger' ones!" The day had been a rare treat, a golden one which would last in the minds of both concerned parties for numerous years to come.

Whether or not I'd in fact been "Jammy" as Andy had joked was quite insignificant. The diminutive number 16, Blue & Olive dry fly had proven its deadly worth on the Hodder's vigorous grayling on a seemingly unwelcoming day which had threatened to turn into a snowstorm.

I was by now somewhat drained by the cold air and earlier exertions yet extremely contented. I drove the car into the inky darkness through the eerie Trough of Bowland towards home. My mind was however already developing a plan for the 'next' visit to that spectacular old stream with great expectancy.

This is the dressing; it is still as deadly today as it was then.

THE BLUE & OLIVE DUN

Hook: 12-20 (fine wire)
Thread: olive waxed
Tail: blue dun cock hackle fibres
Body: grey goose herl, preferably from the wing of a Pink footed goose
Rib: primrose tying silk
Hackles: medium blue dun cock and medium to dark olive cock, twisted through each other

Chapter 7

The rough little becks of Lancashire and Yorkshire have a rugged, timeless beauty.

The Ribble, Hodder, Lune, Greta, Twiss, and Doe; these ancient rivers with equally ancient names originating from bygone eras are as old as the mineral strata which frequently surround them. They can be exceedingly beautiful locations, inspiring wonderment in the lone angler and yet at times mysterious and extremely bleak landscapes.

In such places we occasionally discover crusty local characters, both human and animal alike, with iron wills as hard as the fighting powers of the native trout.

I recall one season, as I wandered down to the River Doe in Yorkshire, I was obliged to ask an elderly lady if she required assistance after observing her beleaguered collie dog wedged tightly against a dry stone wall by a very angry Frisian heifer. For some unidentified reason the beast had taken a rampant dislike to the unfortunate pooch, totally ignoring the woman's rather ignoble (yet quite understandable) cries for it to "Bugger off !" and "Get off home!"

In typically self-governing Yorkshire style, the dog's owner refused my offer. "Oh its okay ta, I'm not going to let 'half a ton of beef burger get the better of me love" she shouted back, trying hard to obviously make light of the current 'sticky' state of affairs. My sympathies however were largely with the bewildered mutt who was by now urgently trying to get away from the belligerent cow that had succeeded in well and truly trapping it into a tightly walled corner of the meadow.

Still, one can only offer so off I tramped down to the beck. Later on, the lady and her dog passed by, seemingly none the worse for their little catastrophe, so at least they did survive the attentions of that unwanted bovine admirer.

It may also seem quite laughable but sheep can also prove rather too friendly at times. I recollect a tall acquaintance of mine, Peter, having to virtually run for his life once when a very maternal 'ewe' (who obviously viewed anglers as an imminent threat to her offspring) decided to put 'Horn-to-Buttocks' in rather dramatic fashion.

My friend was so shook up that even after his bruised 'Gluteus maximus' and ego had healed; it was literally months before he dared venture across that pasture again. Furthermore, he informed me that it was extremely difficult to "leg it" when one is lumbered up with rod, creel, net, an assortment of fly vest gadgetry and heavy chest waders which threaten to pull you down deeper into the muddy pasture.

This is a dubious pleasure that I try to avoid at all costs and is a very good reason why us gritty wild Northern country fly fishers must stay as fit as possible at all times.

Believe me! It's really quite surprising the degree of warp speed a heavily loaded angler can muster up when a psychotic horned inhabitant (with a bad attitude problem!) gets it into its head to commit serious GBH to one's nether regions.

On another occasion Peter gave us both a great belly laugh some time later when he inelegantly stepped off the generally allotted farm track right into a boggy cow patch, which sucked him in like a ravenously unbalanced, organic Hoover with a man-eating grudge.

I'd been nonchalantly chatting to him as we slowly trudged side by side up a steep hillside when I turned to see that he'd suddenly shrunk from his usual six foot plus to less than four foot. Instant horror almost immediately turned to uncontrolled laughter as we realised that, although he wasn't sinking any further, he was quickly beginning to look more like 'Swamp Thing' than a genuine human being.

The more he struggled to get his legs out of this incredibly smelly quagmire the filthier he become. Loyal fly fisher to the end, Peter was still fiercely clutching his precious little split cane rod yet the more he tried to balance himself the more he was forced to stop himself falling by sticking his hands into the obnoxious bog.

What really amazed me though was the strange fact that although he had managed to get the 'orrible muck all over his face and clothing, he STILL had his peaked tweed cap on and more incredibly- it remained in absolutely pristine form.

Trying hard not to completely crack up giggling like some demented schoolgirl, I suggested that we'd need to call for the Farmer's aid and pull him clear with a tractor and chain. This comment only made matters worse, as my slightly mischievous yet well meant comment caused him to flop over again, cackling insanely even further down into the gooey brown crud.

We couldn't speak for laughing and although I was trying hard to pull him out, the complete Fawlty Towers-like countenance of the moment seemed to take the strength from my arms better than any savage illness ever could. By now, my belly and throat were aching so much with laughter that it really hurt and Peter was just the same.

He sure wasn't the sort of thing that you'd want to meet on a cold dark night and now on all fours, looking like a well-dunked victim from Willy Wonker's Chocolate Factory and oh boy-the smell! Yuk! Even the meddlesome cattle, that had now plodded over to watch the fun, seemed to walk away faster than usual after getting a whiff of the action. I don't think they recognised this squelching and incredibly glutinous sight as a human being and without doubt no one could blame them for sloping off when it started to thrash about in its pool of muck.

Finally, not wanting to miss this barmy moment, I told Peter to throw me his pocket camera as he wallowed about, Hippo-style, to record this crazy event which he did. Sadly, the shot wasn't very good but I still grin when I see it. On that memorable day the old gods of fishing laughed at us and we laughed straight back at them.

The countryside may be very beautiful but it's always full of dangers as well. Fortunately, we knew that the above mentioned bog wasn't too deep from past experience yet accidents happen and one always needs to be highly vigilant whilst out on the moors or mountainside. Quicksand is always a possibility in the wilderness so don't take liberties on unknown terrain! If you do then you may not live to tell the tale!

Very odd things occur in the wilderness when we least expect it and the avid dry fly angler sometimes catches more than he bargained for.

Some days prior to Peter's unplanned 'Beauty treatment' in the Hodder swamp, we had been fishing on the River Lune close to Hornby in Lancs. It was a mild mannered morning around early April; one of those silvery days when the promise of good dry fly fishing doesn't seem too far away and although the first swallows had not yet reached the rivers, one or two sand martins were acrobatically strafing the rocky pools busily hunting for emerging duns.

Early season on this lovely river can either mean heavy rain and floods or mild breezy weather with respectable hatches of the Large Dark Olive coming off in profusion. Stone flies too often put in an appearance along with the occasional hatch of assorted Black Gnats on the sunnier days.

It's the same story further up the valley when one reaches the classic, high country Yorkshire streams such as the Rivers Greta, Doe and Twiss.

The main difference between fishing the Lune and the higher limestone becks is one of exposure to the elements. Unfortunately, the wind is usually present on the Lune simply because it's so much bigger. Even on nice sunny days a light breeze can threaten to play havoc with one's line as you struggle to punch it out to risers under the far bank. Furthermore, the Lune can sometimes be a little too popular with the RAF. On one occasion I counted no less than thirteen massive Hercules transporter planes zoom very low over my head as I desperately tried to concentrate on the rising brownies at hand. Half an hour later two ultra noisy Tornadoes nearly pushed me into the swim as they come over a nearby hill like bats out of hell. The day in question was otherwise rather peaceful, even the wind had dropped to an almost imperceptible whisper.

As expected, the LDOs put in the most predominant show. I also spotted a few Iron Blues which failed to attract the trout's immediate interest.

Instinctively, my arm pushed out the little number three, DT floater to a good fish which had suddenly started to hit a few struggling LDOs only some five yards out by a large semi-submerged boulder.

I grimaced as the artificial caught a light puff of breeze and was inadvertently snagged up by the near side of the moss-topped rock. Fortunately, a deft flick of the wrist caused it to drop back into the stream yet the delay in its presentation meant that my would-be quarry had it well and truly 'weighed up' because of the inherent drag factor. Thus, apart from a tiny nip, the fish defiantly rejected the offering without further concern.

At times like this it's all too easy to keep anxiously casting one's fly over the target fish in hope of a better presented cast. However, years of experience has taught me the 'hard way' that it's infinitely wiser to take a break and give the trout chance to recover their, often fickle, confidence or at least time to slightly forget one's clumsily placed effort. Failure to apply this unwritten rule can result in scaring your prey and putting it down for a very long time. Wild browns are highly developed 'feeding machines' that really do learn by their mistakes.

Once they have been agitated by an 'obviously artificial' creation they will frequently let you know. This they usually do by either ignoring your beautifully dressed pattern completely or alternatively, using it as a toy to be generally splashed at, nebbed and head-butted like a beach ball on Torquay sands. If you've ever had such an experience, and many anglers will have, then you will certainly understand the inherent frustration which comes from the situation.

It could be that the run you are fishing is too slow and your leader is glinting with sun light. Then again, it could be 'stream-drag' via bad presentation, too thick a leader or the wrong pattern. Whatever the reason for rejection, the most sensible course of action for the angler is to give the fish a short rest.

Following my unwanted friendship with the rock, I took my own advice and promptly sat on the bank for some three to four minutes.

The time was certainly not wasted as on the very next cast up came the fish. With a golden-flanked splash the LDO imitation was sucked deep under the grey surface film. Without consciously thinking, instinct took over and my right fist pulled firmly into the wild brown beauty.

This nice specimen weighing 1 pound was duly netted after a decent scrap and before long more trout became active thanks to the profusion of fluttering olives now alighting on the river.

I caught a couple more good fish before chancing my luck further downstream. There was though now a slight drawback with the sport which really had to be seen to be believed. A multitude of ravenous sand martins had started to join the aquatic feeding frenzy and before long made their graceful presence known to me, as the only angler in sight, in no uncertain terms.

I'd spotted what appeared to be an excellent fish constantly rising close to my position and made the necessary presentation. Just inches prior to the dressing reaching its intended target a martin swooped down and hovered kestrel-fashion over my fly. Then without further ado, up went the pattern firmly gripped in the bird's beak to a height of some six feet above the water's surface. I could hear my self saying: "No, no-drop it you stupid fool!" as the hungry little creature rose even further into the sky, my line tightening more with each passing second.

I couldn't make it spit out the artificial no matter what. However, with a sigh great of relief from both parties concerned, my feathered friend rejected this obviously highly attractive offering and flew off totally uninjured. I didn't know whether to laugh or cry yet at least I knew that my pattern must have been a damn good imitation of the natural duns on the surface.

Incredibly, five minutes later the very same thing happened again. The fly was cast to a riser, down swooped another martin and 'whoosh,' up went my leader like a magic grey snake into the wild blue yonder. As the bird dropped the pattern I was left thankful that I'd not used a smaller dressing for if I had then the bird could have possibly hooked itself properly.

The 'martin-catching' dressing in question was a variant of the Baigent's Dark Olive. I believe that the late Dr Baigent of Northallerton designed a series of dry patterns which used rather long and stiff game cock hackles. This method enabled the fly to stand well clear of the water giving the dressing a most authentic countenance.

I never knew the good doctor but his overlong hackle idea certainly does appear to attract the fish (and our feathered pals too!)

Although the Baigent's patterns call for a 'Large stiff game cock hackle' I'm personally happier using one which is a teeny bit softer. One of those easily obtained Indian or Chinese game cock capes will allow you to knock up literally hundreds of Baigent-style dressings for a fraction of the price splashed out on the top range 'Stiff' capes. Furthermore, I believe that the softer hackle can lead to improved hooking potential as stiff hackles will at times actually bounce right out of the trout's jaws. I've noticed this accidental rejection occur quite a lot with grayling too which do have small, under-slung mouths.

If you're still unconvinced then you can check it out for yourself with the following test. Dress one tiny dry fly 'fully' with an expensive, stiff hackle. Then tie one with a softer, slightly 'henny' cock hackle. Put them on a flat surface then, with your index finger, gently try to laterally trap them between finger and table top.

Whilst the soft-dressed pattern is relatively easy to capture the stiff one will often be found to reject your advances and spring away. Apply the same basic logic to the stream holding a fat ol' lunker and that ultra expensive, super-duper cape in the tackle shop may not seem quite such a good investment after all!

The tyro angler that's gone and shelled out lots of hard-earned dosh for flashy stiff capes may understandably feel cheated after considering my words yet all is not lost! Stiff, long-hackled capes have their uses.

The main priority with these attractive feathers is to use them with a greater degree of sparseness. Thus, two or three turns may be adequate wherein with the softer hackle fly five or six may prove better.

On fast flows the hackle density question is not quite so crucial. Herein the fish either ignore the dressing completely or alternatively thump into it very fast/hard due to the make or break time factor involved for them.

Naturally, some anglers will cry "Yes, but the stiff-hackled fly floats better!" This doesn't really matter so long as one keeps the dressing well treated with floatant and remembers to throw in a few false-casts now and then to help expel excess moisture. Moreover, just because we may possess a fly that floats like the proverbial champagne cork shouldn't mean that we have to constantly torment the quarry with it. Many anglers would do well to have a fly on that actually needs regular attention simply because this gives the fish a rest and time to recover from our sometimes unrelenting attentions.

Always heed the old maxim: "All that glitters is not gold!" which frequently relates so well to angling/angling equipment issues. Although the ad men will certainly not thank me for raising these matters, do remember this point the next time you are looking at that glossy, fifty quid cape in the tackle shop! Expensive hackles are of course a joy to tie with and do make more flies per feather than their soft-fibre counterparts. However, I firmly believe that they do catch more anglers than fish.

Well as for proof of the pudding? I have to say that my fishing pals and I have been catching quality game fish all season on Lancs/Yorkshire becks with dry flies made from three soft -hackled game cock capes which cost only £1.00 each. Now that's what I call a genuine bargain!

As I stated above, my "martin-catching" pattern was a variant of Baigent's Dark Olive. This I dress with a softer cock hackle and the traditional starling wing material I replace with waterhen (mainly because this was all I had available in my tying bag at the time of creation!)

All in all there are about eleven different Baigent's patterns in the long hackled series. Most sport a body made with stripped peacock quill which gives a nice 'insecty' lifelike appearance.

I hope that old Dr Baigent would forgive me for softening up the hackles on his patterns but this well meant aberration does indeed work well for me personally and has led to the capture of numerous trout and grayling on wild northern streams.

The various colours of hackle and wing materials incorporated in the flies allow the angler to match the hatches of many different insects when dressed from size 20 up to number 12 hooks.

For anyone who cares to have a bash the following Baigent's variants are easy to dress and, because of their larger than normal hackles, a breeze to spot on dark, peat-stained becks.

Finally, do watch out for those greedy martins!

REGAN'S BAIGENT DARK OLIVE

Thread: olive waxed
Hook: 14-18 fine wire
Tail: dark olive cock
Body: stripped peacock quill from 'eye' dyed olive
Wing: Waterhen or coot wing quill
Hackle: long olive cock (of a softer texture than original pattern)

This fly is brilliant in hatches of the: LDO, Olive Upright, Large Spurwing and BWO, at its deadliest from late March to June.

REGAN'S BLACK BAIGENT

Thread: fine black
Hook: 14-18 fine wire
Body: orange floss
Thorax: peacock herl
Rib: peacock herl
Hackle: long black cock

This is useful as a 'fancy 'pattern for grayling when plenty of terrestrial insects hit the stream in high summer.

REGAN'S BROWN BAIGENT

Thread: yellow or brown waxed
Hook: 12-16 fine wire
Tag (optional): gold Lurex
Body: yellow floss or SLF dubbing
Wing: hen pheasant (dressed flat over body)
Hackle: furnace or brown, long in fibre

This is a very useful fly to have on the leader during late summer evenings when Sedges abound. I concur that it may not seem at first glance to be any direct sedge imitation but it does give the right impression to the quarry at these times.

Chapter 8

Numerous centuries ago, a few miles North-East of Preston, Lancashire, the victorious Roman Legions built a defensive horse fort on the chilly banks of the mighty River Ribble. The Latin name for this beautiful watercourse was 'Belisama' and the Romans identified it with their great goddess 'Minerva.'

This wild and isolated outpost was once known as 'Bremetennacum' yet today it sports the name 'Ribchester' wherein a small Roman museum and Bath House are now virtually all that remains to remind us of the proudly disciplined invaders who once repelled fierce, woad-painted, Northern tribes. The local Celtic Brigantes for example gave the straight-laced, Latin aggressors plenty of problems and were never too impressed by their presence in this green land.

Homesick troops must have thought that this was a very austere location when compared to the gentler climes of Mother Rome. However, Caesar's noble legions left these green isles much to the delight of the indigenous peoples with some haste following catastrophic events back in Rome in 410 AD.

The hard-scrapping game fish of the Ribble valley area are still thankfully as wild as ever though, yet it's not too difficult to imagine an off duty centurion enjoying an hour or so hunting out the odd salmon or trout from this lovely river. Without doubt, the stirring sight of a large and highly edible brownie or sea trout, just hovering seductively in the peaty current, would have certainly attracted the attention of many a hungry serviceman flanking the waters.

A Roman road actually ran northwards from Ribchester to a dark and mysterious smaller tributary known as the 'River Hodder.' Thus, any fish-loving legionnaire had two rivers to choose from as the Hodder is only approximately five miles further up the track.

My own adoration of this marvellous, yet frequently quite foreboding spate stream began over twenty years ago. The Hodder has a strange magnetic quality about it that defies conscious logic at times and draws one back to its boulder-strewn banks again and again with the start of each new season. It flows, largely unabated, virtually under the shadow of Longridge Fell in the lovely Forest of Bowland. Originating near Lamb Hill Fell, the Hodder twists and tumbles like a hissing viper into Stocks Reservoir then passes the little towns of Slaidburn, Whitewell and Chipping before eventually spilling out into the Ribble near Great Mitton.

The native salmon and sea trout herein are often larger than one would expect for such a small stream and I have taken my fair share of both over the years. However, as a dry fly fanatic, it's the well-spotted browns and excellent grayling that constantly hold my own attention. The brown trout, whilst not as big as those of the more northerly River Lune, are free-rising given a good head of water is present and the grayling can grow to very good size indeed – I know this personally after numerous 'silver ladies' of around the two and a half pound mark have graced my net!

As well as the neighbourhood browns and grayling, sea trout too can frequently be taken on dry flies. Moreover, this particular species often turns up later in the season when one is expecting to raise a big grayling or two. I have discovered that Hodder sea trout are quite partial to 'grayling fancies' such as The Witch, Red Tag and that old faithful dressing - the Treacle Parkin.

Lusty sport can be had on balmy summer evenings when a plethora of Sherry Spinners conjoin with Pale Wateries and later sedges. I like to carry a selection of patterns to match all perceivable hatches expected on this stream and also a few terrestrial dressings such as ants, beetles etc.

Although they are occasionally rather unloved by a few fly anglers, very large chub often nail one's dry fly when fishing the Hodder.

I affectionately recall one sizzling August evening viewing an unknown fish indulging in an increasing progression of sipping rises under overhanging alders, some ten yards from my casting position. My little 6' 1" stream rod snaked out its no. 3 D/T line straight towards the target. Without a moments warning, the tiny pale midge dressing instantly disappeared under the peat-stained surface film. The rod lashed into a savage arc as the excessive weight out in the current informed me that I'd connected to something rather larger than a mere half pound brownie. As I was using only two pound double-strength leader I couldn't apply much pressure. Meanwhile, my aquatic opponent was boring deeper and deeper towards the riverbed as it stripped yet more line down to the reel's backing.

Attractive possibilities were clogging my mind now. Was this high-speed leviathan a fit grilse, giant grayling, huge brown or lusty sea trout? All these thoughts came to me as I played the beastie, arms now aching into the inky black gloaming. It was hot too, very hot and the pesky local smuts were feasting annoyingly on the sweat, which was now dripping from my face with glee. After what seemed like hours, a large silver shape thankfully bellied into my awaiting net. Imagine my total disappointment as I suddenly realised that my prize 'game' fish was in reality an extra fat 'chub,' not far off double figures in weight! It would have thrilled any course angler but it was not the trophy I'd been expecting on this particular occasion.

From that eventful day many moons ago, numerous big Hodder chub have graced my net. However, so have a plethora of game fish including large browns to two pound plus, sea trout to over six pound and many good grayling to two and a half pound. I've even been known to take my share of Hodder salmon to over sixteen pounds when the season's been a washout with swollen river heights, yet that s another story.

The vast majority of my fish have been grassed on dry flies as this is always my preferred method. For me personally, the dry puts one in closest proximity with the elements, with nature and thus with the total enjoyment of catching lovely wild fish.

By closely imitating the adult 'dry' insect one becomes intimately attuned to the stream and its watery vibrations in a way that chucking in some huge flashy lure connected to an ungainly rod can never match! I have always tied my own patterns too as one can never expect some distant shop to know 'exactly' just what an insect looks like on one's own patch of river.

Browns and grayling coexist well in what seems like perfect unison in the Hodder, although I'm sure that both species do occasionally prey on each others eggs and fry. It's quite common to land both species on the same day along with the odd late-run sea trout and not forgetting of course fat chub too.

The Hodder receives rather mixed hatches, according to the prevailing weather system. During extra stagnant, low water conditions flies may be spare, limited to evening rises. Yet when a good head of water ensues, laced with a modicum of warmish and sunny afternoons, hatches can be overwhelmingly spectacular! All manner of spinners and duns can appear, thus the wise fisherman always stocks up with a good variety of dry imitative dressings plus a few tiny 'fancies' – just in case the going gets tough.

In my experience most Hodder browns range from about six to ten ounces with a smattering going to one and a half pounds, larger specimens do exist yet they are rare. However, I have always believed strongly that this river could produce a record-breaking grayling as I've landed so many over the two pound mark. They fight like tigers - using that huge dorsal fin to very good 'current-flanking' effect. The biggest specimen grayling frequently turn up at the start of the trouting season, yet August to late October is probably the most enjoyable time to catch them, depending of course on prevailing weather conditions. They can either be stupid, hitting one's fly at almost every cast, or alternatively incredibly fussy refusing most offers set before them. When they get ultra selective and start defying even a size 24 dressing they can be real little devils to tempt. Two choices usually face the angler given this situation. One can either 'stick-it-out' and discover an attractive pattern that they will take or stroll off up stream to find another shoal. Frequently the latter approach is more prudent as this at least gives the fish a rest (there's never any point in thrashing the water to foam in frustration anyway) and this saves one's energies until more cooperative grayling stocks are located.

The Hodder is almost always stained with peat, especially after a small spate. If the stream is too high then dry fly can become difficult with the water becoming a dirty chocolate hue, yet one may take a fish or two in quieter, shallow pools of the main current. On many occasions I have taken fish in high but slack pools behind rocks as the later olives hatched out – even on large pools when the huge autumn salmon have been waiting, like silver torpedoes, to run further upstream.

I find that the best time to catch summer trout on dry is when the river is recovering two or three days after a small flood. This is particularly true subsequent to a long period of drought. The extra water always stirs up a multitude of aquatic life forms and makes for aggressively feeding game fish; ergo successful angling ultimately follows close behind. If the Hodder is excessively low, clear and hot when one arrives then the evening rise is usually the best bet. No point in wasting valuable concentration on spooky fish that can see (and feel) one before we spot them!

As each Hodder season passes it strengthens my belief in angling with ultra small rods (my current home-made favourite is but 5' 2"), light double-strength leaders, and tiny dry patterns which actually 'look' like the insects found on the river.

The Hodder can never be taken for granted yet for the committed dry fly fanatic on the right day it is as good as any other river in the land. Its Lancashire scenery with majestic oaks, alders and ash blended into awesome slabs of ancient grey rock is marvellous too!

Nothing much has changed around her since the first Romans surveyed the place many centuries ago- and that's the way I like it!

For the dry fly angler one word sums it all up – Home!

Two good dry fly patterns for the River Hodder

GENERAL DRY OLIVE VARIENT

Hook: 14-18 light wire.
Thread: olive waxed.
Tail: blue dun cock.
Body: grey-blue mole, rabbit or hare, dubbed.
Wing: Waterhen or coot split and advanced.
Rib: (optional) pale yellow tying thread.
Hackle: natural pale red or light ginger cock.

PAT'S PALE GRAYLING MIDGE

Hook: 16-24 light wire.
Thread: fine white.
Tail: cream dun.
Body: pale grey rabbit fur, dubbed.
Wing: none.
Rib: none.
Hackle: palest gin

Chapter 9

Although there can never be any proper substitute for personal experience hands on at the waterside, a certain part of the inherent wisdom of the dry fly fisher's art can perhaps be easiest to understand via tales from the riverbank undertaken by others.

The following story which is, like others in this book, based on true events may sharpen the appetite of the novice or experienced angler alike.

A lone curlew's sad cry echoed through the limestone valley as the earlier mist began to clear.

With a sense of timeless continuity, the old dry fly fisherman's weather-beaten fingers deftly put their finishing touches to the diminutive blood knot. Long past experience told him that his newly chosen dry fly pattern was 'The One' that would finally tempt that gently rising leviathan, now residing under the far bank. To the untrained eye, there was no apparent rush in the angler's dexterous yet easygoing movements. However, his great familiarity with his craft masked a certain urgency originating from the sure knowledge that his chosen quarry would not be available for much longer.

He knew only too well that time was of the essence. Before long the brown trout would have had its fill of the tasty floating morsels presented by the evening rise and returned to the watery depths.

With head held low, the angler's eyes narrowed into piercing slits as he focused intently on the semi-visible trout. The double taper number 3 fly line whipped out through the angler's rod rings like a coiled viper hunting its unsuspecting target.

A golden myriad of tiny flying insects silently danced in the pale evening sunlight over the boulder-strewn riverbank, like miniature ballerinas seeking to please a captivated audience.

As if in a supporting act, a large swarm of Sherry Spinners joined in the aerial display; their graceful swooping and falling mating preoccupation rendering them totally oblivious to the almost motionless yet deadly aquatic predator lurking patiently below.

The evening was quite placid yet one unlucky spinner, instantly caught in a light puff of wind coming off the green meadows behind, suddenly realised that she was flying much too close to the beck's watery pull. Subsequently, milliseconds later she ended up pathetically struggling to no avail in the peat-stained surface film.

Devoid of any hope, this pitiful Sherry Spinner, by now waterlogged and dying, slowly drifted downstream past the overhanging branches of an ancient solitary hawthorn. Her final half-hearted attempts to prolong her all too painfully short existence did not however go entirely unnoticed.

A long dark shadow, just inches below and slightly to the right hand side of her position, kept perfect synchronistic pace with the hapless fly, monitoring every last movement of her twitching red body.

Meanwhile, other waterside residents were also keeping busy. A highly active yellow wagtail narrowly missed the floundering spinner. The bird's sharp beak snapping like an irate clam as she hastily zigzagged through the translucent-winged spinner swarm above. Her skilful efforts successfully finished off two other unfortunate, yet previously still airborne, spinners instead.

This gaily-plumed waterside resident had been on the wing all afternoon. Olive Uprights, Blue winged olives, assorted black gnats, stoneflies and a plethora of midge life meant that her crop was by now getting rather full. Greedy little nestlings though required sufficient nourishment and the rocky beck supplied a huge wealth of insect choice for experienced parental wagtails.

The sudden metallic blue and orange flash of a super-fast passing kingfisher caused the wagtail to almost fall off her rocky perch. Mr Kingfisher had also been feeding, albeit further upstream. Not on insects but on the small silver fry and brown minnows that teemed in their millions under the old, lichen-encrusted stone bridge.

By now, all movement had left the Sherry Spinner's body. She was merely one of hundreds, who would that evening become part of the eternal dietary food chain of the little Yorkshire beck.

The irresistible push of the current detached the trapped and lifeless insect from a small hawthorn twig touching the water's surface. As the little corpse drifted onwards, her end was finally secured. However, her departure was not completely in vain.

A sudden explosive silver flash parted the mirrored film as the big brown trout turned, rose and clamped his waiting jaws around the unfortunate spinner.

He wasn't really that hungry as he'd been feasting on various duns earlier that afternoon. The stream held rich pickings yet Sherry Spinners were hard to refuse for they tasted so good and were a synch to catch. Duns, on the other hand, soon dried themselves off and flew away. Unless of course the day was hot and still, making it harder for them to escape the stickier surface film of the beck!

Seemingly now unaware of his own mortality, in the heat of the moment the fish turned once more to intercept yet another Sherry Spinner which had just landed eleven inches in front of his razor-toothed neb.

With a quick flick of his powerful tail the trout moved into taking position then, without any fuss, confidently sipped in the floating insect. In an instant the fish realised his fatal mistake. He'd fallen prey to the largest predator of the beck.... Man!

White fly line ripped through the previously tranquil waters. The diminutive six-foot midge rod suddenly bent almost double, as it connected the old hunter to his well-chosen quarry.

Ten yards of loosely coiled line flew out from between the angler's fingers at lightening speed as the large brownie made a determined bid to obtain freedom.

Three times the fish leapt acrobatically into the air, head shaking savagely like a thing possessed, as it tried to shed the tiny artificial fly now firmly attached to its scissors.

The old angler however never wavered. His long-experienced hands were now in full control of the situation and soon the trout drifted, fully beaten, into the waiting landing net. All was not however lost for this particular fish.

Soon the trout gained its previous strength, as the angler gently held it horizontally in the beck's healing current. With a deft flick of its huge tail the big fish detached itself from warm fingers and headed across the beck to find quiet sanctuary under the submerged roots of an ancient ash tree. Before long the trout's experience would be forgotten, with recovery complete.

At nearly two and a half pounds it was indeed an excellent specimen. The angler already had three other decent trout in his creel that would prove sufficient for several tasty meals. This hard-scrapping beauty could therefore go back and grow into a three-pounder!

The haunting screech of a tawny owl perched high in a nearby alder tree informed the old man that darkness was fast approaching. Enough light would however be available to see the track back to home through the woods. The sky was clear and tonight the waxing yellow moon cast long still shadows across the windless fields surrounding the beck.

Trout had now stopped rising, albeit for the odd greedy tiddler, and millions of microscopic reed smuts plagued the old man, as they danced annoyingly around his bearded face. He couldn't however help admiring the delicate gossamer wings of the beautiful little Sherry Spinner that had just landed on his sleeve. In an instant, it flew away across the beck to join its many peers that were now swarming several yards above the glistening surface film. Some would survive to lay their eggs and thus carry on the species. Others would end up food for the beck's hungry inhabitants. This was the way of the stream, the way it has always been and the way it always will.

Red orange and purple streaks lashed the halcyon evening sky now as the angler reluctantly made his last cast. He was rather tired after his afternoon excursion but he wasn't complaining.

On the contrary, sport had been brisk thanks to the later falls of Sherry Spinners. Just as he was about to trim his fly from its leader, a sudden erratic splash, only three yards from his position, caused him to jump.

Unable to resist the temptation, the old man quickly dried off his artificial and with a clever side flick placed the fly into the general direction of the rising trout. Although the failing light was now making it difficult for him to see, he knew that his fly wasn't far off target.

The angler's heart missed a beat as the brownie instantly nailed the dressing. It didn't feel like a giant fish yet it made off like a bullet, fly reel now lurching as it bore deep for the safety of the riverbed.

Collecting his wits, the old man stepped into a better fighting position nearly stumbling on a large slippery rock in the process. Suddenly the gyrating trout exploded high into the air, showing its lithe red-spotted flanks, and threw off the irritating barbless hook.

Once long ago in his fish hungry youth such a loss would have been most disconcerting. Today however the angler simply smiled to himself philosophically. He knew that there would be other days, other evening rises when 'Lady Luck' would be on his side.

Mist now formed a whisper soft white carpet over the far bank side. A fluttering bat gorged her self, wheeling and turning, into the thick clouds of pale midges.

The same lone curlew had returned to the limestone valley, its eerie cry now appearing to summon in the growing darkness.

A shining full moon was now high above the treetops as the old man, creel firmly on back, climbed the last farm gate for the comforting lights of home.

He felt an icy shiver go through his bones as he peered into the darkening sky at the first bright stars. It was getting quite cold and thoughts of a nice mug of steaming hot tea were paramount in his mind.

Now, only the babbling rush of water cascading over unstable shingle and the rare sound of a solitary otter, hunting for his nightly feed, would disturb the tranquillity of the little beck.

Very soon silence would reign supreme until the coming of tomorrow's sun.

Chapter 10

The following also relates to true life and I include it in an attempt to yet again impart the magical art of the dry fly towards anyone with an inclination into this most natural and instinctive branch of the game.

It was the end of August and all we had been granted by the weather gods for several weeks was lots of rain and wind. Still, I thought, I'll have a trip to the river and see what's doing. When I got there the Hodder was up and very coloured. First impressions told me that the only people who would have any sport would be the salmon and sea- trouters with either a spinner or worm.

Above: nice water for dry fly fishing on the Hodder.

As I had travelled with my son (who was with me to take photos of local butterflies for his Lepidoptera website) over thirty five miles from home I didn't feel like just running off when faced with this big flood. Not to be daunted, I put up my six foot midge rod and tied on a red tag.

Surprisingly, before long I managed to rise a fish on the lip of a smooth fast run which head-butted my fly without getting a proper hold.

Something told me to change the dressing quick so on went a trusty BWO and on the second cast the fish hit the fly hard. It turned out to be a nice silvery grayling of about twelve ounce which I gently returned to the pool unharmed. My hopes and confidence changed dramatically with this fish and before long several more nice Silver ladies graced my net.

The successful dry fly flood technique was to throw a short line up stream no more than about ten yards as most of the fish where very close into my bank, avoiding the main thrust of the spate. Takes were positive and not the sort of half-hearted nips that can be so frustrating on low, clear conditions.

Later in the afternoon a salmon angler came down to the water yet he had no success with his brightly-coloured Flying C lure.

I almost felt guilty at having such good sport on this flood with the tiny BWO when conditions seems to demand huge metal lures and worming tackle for big migratory species. I ended up with six excellent Hodder grayling which is not a massive catch by any means but considering the adverse river condition was extremely pleasing. I also lost several fish and they all took the BWO dressing. Two, well over the pound mark, were kept for tea and they tasted better than most trout.

The point of this little tale is that one should never pack up and go home as there is nearly always a possibility of some sport - even in the most seemingly impossible of conditions.

September browns on the River Wenning can be elusive to catch yet the rewards speak for themselves.

It's never easy fishing a new stretch of water especially in late summer when, like organic knives, the nettles along with unsympathetic thistles and brambles threaten the unwary angler who has taken a wrong turn into one of our British summertime jungles. And please don't make the mistake of thinking that such places don't exist for I can assure you - they certainly do.

Some stretches of the Wenning cannot be described as a fly-fishers dream, simply because of the great amount of overhanging trees which try to snap one's leader at every other cast. Sport can be had though, albeit with the need for great care and dexterity.

On one occasion, after fighting my way through the Vietnamese-like mass of undergrowth into a decent looking little pool, I noticed a sparse hatch of Medium Olives. Positioning myself into a good mid-stream casting spot I succeeded in raising the nearest taker on a dry dun pattern, which was mouthed by the trout then instantly rejected with playful disgust.

The olive hatch petered out as soon as it had started and rises quickly ceased. The odd stone-fly and sedge that landed on the surface were arrogantly ignored by the Trout. However, all was not lost as a swarm of Great Red Spinners promptly had the fish nicely on the fin once again.

I quickly tied on a dry pattern which instinctively felt right and was soon rewarded with my first Wenning brownie of the late afternoon. It wasn't a monster but fought like a tiger on my six foot midge rod and splashed about all over the pool. I returned this fish promptly, dried the fly and cast again to another riser over to my right, tucked in under an overhanging oak branch. The spinner drifted slowly over her waiting neb, then 'wham' she was on and thrashing about energetically like the last one.

Unlike the darker late-season browns of the Rivers Doe and Twiss, these plump Wenning fish are very shiny and shot through with marvellous colours spaced with exquisite vermillion red spots. Pound for pound their fighting qualities are on a par with the scrappers I've previously hooked in the various stretches of the Lune (and this includes daytime caught sea trout on the dry fly too.)

A long cast upstream produced my third fish which was the best (estimated at just under a pound.) I lost a big one which was around the pound and a half class earlier at the net. All were caught on the same spinner dressing. Soon the spinners disappeared and the river was, apart from the odd call of a lone dipper, once again strangely silent. Night approached and it was time to head for the safe lights of home.

Although sometimes hard work, the inexplicable magic of such beautiful little streams like the Wenning must never be underestimated. They are well worth the effort involved for the dedicated dry-fly angler who wants to find exciting light-line sport, intermixed with wild, North Country natural grandeur.

Although admittedly not a fully imitative dressing, other anglers may be interested in tying the ultra simple (yet quite deadly) pattern mentioned below. The dressing is as follows:

THE WENNING SPINNER

Hook: 16-14 up-eyed fine wire.
Silk: fine grey
Body: greyish brown silk or floss
Wing: none
Hackle: natural medium red cock or ginger

 I believe that this fly could be improved with the addition of a few red cock hackles as a tail although my original did not have them built in. The natural insect has very long tails indeed and is popular with the feeding Trout throughout the day.

Chapter 11

I have frequently asked the following question to local game anglers – "Yes we know it holds 'salmon' - but what about the 'trout' of the River Lune? This honest enquiry has often been greeted with either total disinterest or a lacklustre shrug of the shoulders.

Oddly, many stretches of the River Lune are seriously neglected by trout fishing enthusiasts yet prove to be most popular with the salmon and sea trout brigade. This is strange as the whole system is brilliant for large trout and affords the naturalist angler with the opportunity to catch perhaps his/her best wild specimen.

The silvery waters on the beautiful River Lune, the home of magnificent wild trout, are some of the most productive and eye-catching places to fish a dry fly in the British Isles. Admittedly, these Lune stretches may be larger and less tree-lined in some places than many of the smaller spate streams yet they do produce fine specimens that fight like tigers all the way to the net.

After seeing it with my own eyes over many seasons, I have to reiterate that many aspirant trouters have originally made the big mistake of using too much heavy gear like large ungainly reservoir rods, overtly thick fly lines and terribly over-dressed flies when attempting to catch these wily spate stream trout so they have possibly been put off due to this error. Many of these disenchanted anglers then choose to sign up to the 'Chuck it and chance it' game of chasing migratory fish with flashy spinners, worms or huge so-called 'flies' that look more like something off your granny's Xmas tree or even resort to the 'charms' of hunting down rainbows in man-made stocked lakes.

Alternatively, I have had the very good fortune over the years to have helped one or two truly nature-loving anglers get into the highly addictive yet minority cult of the dry fly - people who were initially in grave danger of resorting to the clumsier angling games as mentioned above instead of the great finesse of the tiny imitative dry fly.

Unhappily many of today's anglers have little feasible notion that fly fishing is 'supposed' to be about imitating the quarry's diet and this ancient skill seemingly belongs to only a few devoted anglers who have the inherent passion and desire to study their prey and its diet in such detail.

My son Kyle is also now a keen naturalist with interests in plant life and insects etc. He recently caught his first Lune trout on a dry fly which weighed in at 1lb 5oz. It would be nice to see more youngsters take up the noble art of the naturalistic fly fisher. The future of our sport lies in the hands of the next generation and it is up to us to show them the way whenever possible.

I must reiterate then that on the northern becks the effective dry fly flood method is to cast a short line upstream no farther than about ten yards as most of the fish can be extremely close into your own position. Takes that occur are positive affairs and not the sort of lackadaisical pecks that can be so exasperating for the angler in lower, clear water flows.

Yes, salmon and sea trout fishers may sometimes seem to gang up on the riverbank after good floods yet they may have little or no success with their massive metal armoury of Toby or Mepps lures and other such frantically gyrating devices. At such times excellent sport with miniature dries can be had when conditions would seem to command the use of these enormous metal lures or perhaps bunches of lobworms on a meat hook for nomadic bars of silver.

Countless times I have ended up with first-rate bags of excellent grayling or brown trout, which considering the adverse flood river conditions proved to be particularly pleasing indeed. Never ever give up hope and rush off to the car too quickly as there is always a chance of a few nice fish - even in the most seemingly discouraging of flood conditions. I would say that the only time a torrent leaves me feeling beaten is when it is so huge that large trees and dead sheep start drifting past and getting in the way; yet even then there can sometimes be a quiet pool to utilise away from the main force of the torrent.

Medium spates and especially ones in hot weather can often afford the best opportunity for the trouter to make a good catch as at these times the fish are enthusiastic to attack every morsel that passes their position.

I can never reiterate enough though that wading into such flood waters is fraught with great danger and the wise angler stays well away from the water in such conditions. The best and most expensive neoprene waders will 'not' save your life if an apparently safe gravel shelf decides to crumble away under you during a spate. Furthermore, it has to be said that wading actually alarms more fish than it catches as many good specimens will be very close to your position in the less turbulent waters.

Above: the author fishing the Lune in Lancashire.

Chapter 12

There's a certain mystery for fishing unknown waters at times and it's only human nature to want to know what is around the next bend in the river. This childlike wonderment has I believe very ancient roots in our psyche.

The earliest Celtic immigrants to these isles regarded boundaries of any kind as being at very least special places and ultimately as sanctified areas. The perceptible line where ocean met sky, waterway crossed land and even the space just above a steed's head; all were seen as divinely-related areas. I feel the same can be said about that wonderful and inexplicable realm which is the surface film of a moorland stream. Here exists the magical air/water boundary where the elements of wild nature conjoin.

For many of us resilient souls, wet fly or gold-head nymph can never truthfully match the unrestrained, innocent wonder that is gleaned from a vigorous trout or grayling sipping down a tiny dry fly. Could it be that with the beginning of competitive (how many fish can one haul out within a set period) approach which is match fishing, numerous fly anglers are losing sight of what our form of sport is (or should be) all about?

Perhaps I am old-fashioned but I still prefer to take one nice fish on the surface imitation to five on a wet fly or nymph. Furthermore, over the years I have taken many superb grayling, trout and other species exclusively on dry patterns when other anglers have struggled close by with fancy, subsurface creations! This is not to say that the later methods don't work well at times because they of course do.

At the end of the day I suppose it's all about what gives the most satisfaction, what feels right. Nevertheless the 'numbers game' state of mind is I feel not what true fly-fishing is really about. Follow that debatable and somewhat covetous path and you will sooner rather than later finish up pulling fish out by the score and mislay that great sense of nature-based mystery that the sport is supposed to be all about. Surely if we want to catch vast amounts of fish we should use a trawl net or a bunch of maggots?

We must never allow our extraordinary 'art,' which connects us on various levels to the intimate balance of nature, to lose its rhythmical aspect, for without such consideration we lose sight of the true beauty of angling with the fly. A boat load of stocked rainbow trout ripped out of a lake at great speed on a regular basis will never stay in the mind and satisfy the spirit as will the memory of that quiet evening rise when one or two healthy grayling gave great sport to the lone angler on a tiny rain-fed stream in august.

One thing is certain when it comes to hunting wild spate stream fish with a dry fly, no one ever caught them by staying at home in the armchair. However, the armchair, or perhaps I should say the fly-dressers chair, is the realm of imagination and the place wherein all manner of weird and wonderful patterns are born. Never be afraid to experiment with your dressings as happy accidents are the basis of many a successful and deadly fly. You don't need to spend a fortune on fancy fly dressing equipment like vices and the like or materials either and much of the gear which we see in catalogues or shops at greatly inflated prices is without doubt superfluous.

A strong little vice will not set you back hundreds of pounds and if it does then perhaps you have fallen for the expertise of tackle manufacturers' marketing techniques rather than followed your inherent common sense. One thing though that is quite critical is a good pair of small, sharp and fine – pointed scissors. Some years ago when I ran fly-dressing classes one of the most frustrating things for my students was found to be in them trying to use clumsy scissors that failed to do the most important thing – cut delicate materials on tiny dry fly hooks without chewing them to pieces. Extremely small hackle pliers are also a most indispensable item that can wind on a hackle down to a size 32, fine-wire hook.

The vice must also be able to handle small hooks yet I reiterate that spending a vast sum on such an item is rather ridiculous. £10 – 15 spent on a new vice should be more than enough money to get you into the swing of dressing good quality flies and nice little streamside vices that you can take with you to the river cost even less. I have used a Weaver ultimate type 1 vice for many years and it's still going strong although today one would cost I believe in the region of £50.00. If it suddenly falls to pieces then I shall expect to get a new vice for considerably less as they are so inexpensive these days.

Materials are incredibly easy to obtain. I have just brushed a bag full of grey rabbit fur from the family pet that is just going into his winter moult. Old Colin never complained about this theft and in fact seemed to actually enjoy his cosmetic grooming experience, at least as much as any posh lady being pampered under a hairdryer in a classy beauty salon. This material will make literally hundreds of natural coloured dry fly bodies and cost me nothing.

So long as one is not squeamish road kills can be another valuable source of prime materials for the frugal dresser. Everyday fresh starling, blackbird, squirrel and other assorted unfortunate victims end up in the gutter and there seems little point in wasting such functional fur and feather. Pet dogs and cats also are a good resource for furs and if you know bird breeders or anyone who keeps poultry you are laughing all the way to the fly vice

The drabber and ultimately more seemingly boring the colours are for your materials the better. Wild trout and grayling desire mainly subdued dressings that imitate the natural dull-coloured river insects so greys, blacks, browns, pale olives etc are what you are looking for.

If you need to replicate somewhat more colourful insects like say the Yellow May Dun or some of the brighter spinner bodies then various dyes are easily obtainable from tackle suppliers or even your local hardware shop.

An elderly pragmatic fly dresser once said to me that he never actually spent anything on materials as all he required was found either in his back garden or from plucking the carpet in his front room. The thrifty dresser can then utilise the hairs on his beard to fashion a superb gnat's body or the moulted neck feather of a ginger bantam cock to roll a lovely sedge wing. Put the word around that you are looking for such materials and before you know it you will be inundated with kind relatives etc giving you balls of wool and old fur coats. And never dismiss the common budgerigar as this pet can provide a constant source of excellent feathers. The duller barred neck and head hackles are brilliant for adding a nice twist of grizzled effect to dry flies and this bird is sorely neglected by many tiers, which is quite surprising considering how common it is.

Try also a few turns of moulted white hackle from a budgie's chest for pale coloured moth imitations in the warm summer evenings and yellow ones to again match the Yellow May Dun. Admittedly, they are a soft textured feather and require the back up of a little twist of same coloured cock hackle but they can and do add a good action which your quarry will find irresistible at times. Just one or two turns of budgie in front of your regular cock hackle will do the trick, light and easy does it, and may make all the difference on the day.

Yes, finding free materials is all part of the enjoyment of creating effective dry flies that will usually look much more natural than ugly shop-bought affairs.

The cult and it really is a cult, of the dry fly is something that can and does change a person forever.

Whether one is fishing a beautiful rain-fed river or dressing flies in the warmth and comfort of home once the art is taken up and the 'bug' gets hold then life will never be the same again.

Chapter 13

Wading can at a minority of times be a necessary evil when fishing the spate streams. However, by and large it does more harm than good. This is a point that can and should be constantly reiterated. Furthermore, angling advertisers/manufacturers must accept some for the responsibility for encouraging the more naïve to believe that unless they can get in the river at chest depth, without the need for a snorkel, they will not catch anything worth the trouble. Nothing could in fact be further from the truth.

This is not an exaggeration either for many a good spate stream run can be and is completely ruined by thoughtless fools that rush into the heart of prime game fishing country and literally scare the hell out of everything that was previously feeding there, blissfully undisturbed by man.

Highly oxygenated animated water of less than six inches deep can hold big trout and grayling and the wise angler always keeps this in mind. I think that many anglers are more interested in actually casting their lines as far as possible than catching the fish close to their own bank. Moreover, many seem to be more engrossed in the performance of their luxurious boron rods or nice fancy new neoprene chest waders than the location of the wonderful fish they are supposed to be seeking to catch. Sadly, years of observation of both our wily quarry and clumsy distance casting deep wading anglers bear out this belief.

Without doubt there are times that one has to carefully get into the stream and wade over to positions wherein huge lunkers are rising. This goes without question, yet I would be rich if I have earned a quid for every time I had seen the more inconsiderate fishermen just wade right through a shallow pool of eagerly feeding trout or grayling shoal to get their flies to swing around some distant rock in the stream.

The above is particularly true on our smaller becks wherein fish can see the approach of an angler with greater ease. Although still risking fish scare one may get away with wading deep on large flows but the diminutive, more concisely structured runs will have trout fleeing like rabbits if you just crash into the water like a possessed dolphin. Think carefully before you wade is the main thing to remember.

Using one's natural auditory faculty is also a prime requisite on the spate streams as on cooler blustery days, especially in early spring when the glass is falling, fish can be hard to spot with the eyes.

Never ever discount the inherent ability of your ears to tell you where fish are rising when the river's surface is ruffled. Learn to trust them implicitly as you do your eyes for they are an ancient part of your hunting equipment which Mother Nature in her great wisdom has provided you with to place food on your table.

It is surprising in fact almost awe-inspiring how accurate hearing can be in pinpointing a rising fish in a stormy beck covered in waves. Once the knack has been properly learnt via personal riverside experience you can often place your dressing right in front of a feeding riser, even though you have not actually seen where it's taking the natural flies coming down the stream.

I fondly recall one notable example of this interesting phenomenon which I gained on the River Lune back in the early 1980s.

It was a particularly raw March day when rather than stay at home like most sensible souls I had decided to make the long journey to the windswept river.

I was impatient to have a crack at the early season browns of this river which can be hard to temp at the best of times yet quite foolhardy when the Large Dark Olives start coming off the surface in profusion before the first showers of April.

Pulling into the car park above the river I had mixed feelings. On one hand I had the place to myself which was great with only a few noisy oystercatchers and curlews for company; however the water looked extremely uninviting with a strong northerly gale ripping across the surface making the stream look more like a Welsh storm beach than a Lancashire beck.

I tackled up my trusty six foot fly rod with a number three double taper line and set off to walk the three quarters of a mile to the end of the stretch.

I have to say that spotting any fish daft enough to rise to duns in this tremendous swell seemed ludicrous and largely a waste of time. I was as usual desperate to satisfy my usual dry fly addiction so I persisted for about an hour, looking intently into the wild foam-tossed surface for signs of life. None where seen.

Then it happened. I was beginning to walk back towards the car park area with disillusionment threatening to creep in. My focus was on the rocky ground under my feet, not on the water where it really should have been. Suddenly, to my side I heard a welcome splash out in the windy surface and without stopping to think about it I instantly and instinctively pitched out my fly into the waves.

Less than three seconds later another splash indicated that a good Lune trout had savaged my dressing and before long line was being ripped through my fingers at a rate of knots. The fish, which weighed in at one and a half pounds, fought well seeking to throw my fly with a series of acrobatic leaps and some minutes later I had it confined to the safety of my net. With the wind in my face which was carrying some cold drizzle and the efforts of this fish I was quite breathless but wanted more of the same as soon as possible.

I trusted my auditory faculties once again and a little while later I heard another splatter, approximately fifteen yards out into the beck, which I cast towards. For a second time a good fish instantly nailed my imitation and soon I had him in the creel.

In between hearing these two fish I tried a few blind casts out into the turbulent foam yet nothing rose to my efforts. The point is that instinct and timing ensured that I placed the fly at precisely the correct place without the advantage of visual substantiation. The targets had been pinpointed exactly under adverse weather conditions without the use of the eyes.

Some may of course claim this to just be a happy angling stroke of luck yet I can assure doubters that the very same experience has occurred too many times over the years to be put down to simple coincidence. Nature has provided the hunting dry fly angler with senses that are in principal just embryonic in most mortals.

These precious instincts are honed, via quiet personal experience in all conditions on the river, and evolve if we only bother to let them. They will never develop properly in noisy crowds of incessantly chatting fisherman who are more interested in the latest football scores or price of a holiday abroad, rather than the quest for untamed fish on the dry.

No, the lone angler or at least the one with a shrewd companion who knows plenty about the significance of riverside silence and stealth will always be the individual to sharpen his/her intrinsic skills into something greater than the norm.

Actually this gift, and gift it is for sure, surpasses the sport of angling and filters through into everything the practitioner of the noblest art ever does in life almost to the point of elitism. Similar claims may be made by the advocates of say martial arts like karate or kung fu who have been reaping the supplementary life benefits of their art for many years in everyday life.

It almost seems that the efforts one puts into such things are in fact reaped in unexpected ways that are not always apparent to us at the inauguration of our first interest in these events. Wits and instincts that our ancient ancestors took for granted are truly sharpened and these filter right back down into our normal daily existence, which can only be a good and incredibly positive thing in itself.

Chapter 14

Again, speaking of the hearing facility having precedence over vision, the night angler will have some appreciation of what I am talking about herein.

The solitary late night sea trouter casting his flies into the beck's unknown darkness has to rely to a large extent on his ears rather than his visual faculty. The sense of hearing then combines with the deeper spatial awareness which starts to take over when vision is impaired by darkness at these times.

Call it the inner sixth sense if you like but when the normal everyday faculties are impaired unexplained things really start to happen. One then starts to place trust in instinctive feelings rather than what can be seen. Some go on to develop this talent via long practice while others fail miserably and are doomed to a persistent series of line tangles, accidents and frustration.

The dry fly angler can also take good advantage of this sixth sense when darkness falls onto the summer river.

In order to achieve the best possible chance of a fish one is at times forced into fishing into the night and this is especially so during periods of drought and daytime heat. Given the choice I personally prefer to be able to actually see my dry fly on the surface as opposed to fishing into the night.

When the river is dried out on its bones and the day has been a real scorcher, or 'stinking hot' as colloquially stated by farmers in parts of Lancashire, in the months from June to September then the fish tend to become very lethargic unless the rains bring a good flush of new richly oxygenated water to the beck.

Even the excitedly anticipated and greatly overestimated 'Evening rise' may at these times just not occur to any worthwhile degree as we would hope. This usually means that the fish have become nocturnal in their feeding habits and shun 99% of all daylight foraging. Of course this is of no consolation to the spate stream angler who only wants to see trout take his fly off the surface yet there can be certain advantages for the hardier soul who wishes to persist into the gloaming.

For one thing line strength can be increased substantially as night feeders do accept thicker leaders than the daylight fish, who would run like terrified rabbits at the sight of such dense mono. They will also take larger flies that again would have them scared witless on such low thin runs during the day. I would urge anyone wanting to fish into the night with a dry fly to definitely increase the strength of their leader because one can never be certain just what will attach itself the end of your line. Furthermore, even small beck brownies become much more aggressively hard-hitting in the darkness and smash takes are not unheard of so please do not take any chances- step up your leader before you tackle them.

Also trout and other species do travel into extremely shallow runs during the night to reap the harvest of late olives so long casting is frequently not an essential practice.

Many times one can be stood in water less than knee depth at night several yards away from one's own bank and hear fish rising happily behind your position. Furthermore, the sudden unexpected knock against one's leg from a large salmon or sea trout moving upstream can be quite alarming at two in the morning. I speak from personal experience.

Yes, at night fish can be more forgiving and I would say that careful, even clumsy, wading may be tolerated by them to some extent that would otherwise never be accepted during the harsh light of a blistering summer's day.

I recall one particular nocturnal jaunt I enjoyed on the River Hodder some seasons ago.

The day was hot, very hot that August afternoon. The river gauge indicated that the stream was about nine inches below summer level and that if I had been in possession of my senses I would have not even bothered to make the trip to the river in the first place.

Even walking down the steep hill through the woods was hard work as the temperatures soared into the high eighties. With sweat dripping off my face I got to the old fishing hut at the edge of the stream. The rocks on the far side of the river which were usually submerged were baked dry and exposed by the ferocious sun.

Nevertheless, even though it was exceptionally low the watercourse was so beautiful with huge overhanging oaks and alders swaying and creaking gently in the light afternoon zephyr. A lightening fast blue and orange kingfisher streaked past me like a little jet, flying rapidly downstream. He had a tiny fish in his beak so at least one fisherman, albeit a feathered one, could claim success already.

I unlocked the door of the hut. Pulling off my trusty wicker creel, which as well as fish often carries pounds of sloe or elderberries for wine making, I leaned against the side of the hut to get my breath back after the long trek to the river.

It was just so hot with my shirt sticking to my back and yet a feeling of anticipation was in the air.

I decided to take it easy for five minutes and have a quick sandwich with a welcome drink of juice so I pulled out an old deckchair that some kindly fisherman had left in the hut and plonked my self down to watch the river for any signs of life.

A myriad of tiny pale insects, probably midges, buzzed incessantly around the knotted old twin-trunked sycamore in front of me yet I saw nothing but a few small fry move on the ultra thin surface film. It was not going to be easy to catch anything under these adverse conditions.

Putting together my midge rod I then tied a small black terrestrial beetle imitation on a size 18 hook to my fine six and a half foot tippet and set off to seek out some deep streamed runs. I figured that any fish feeling peckish would perhaps be at least trying to find some shelter from the blazing early afternoon sun under overhanging boughs. On hot days they wait at times in such positions in the hope of a few dozy caterpillars or other hapless insects caught by a puff of breeze falling with a plop into the water.

An old reddish rock on the far side of the stream caught my attention. Without doubt a good fish was rising behind this big boulder at a rate of about three times a minute.

Instantly my little beetle flicked out into the current and came trundling nicely past the fish, which nonchalantly head-butted my dressing as if to say "no chance mate – try again".

So try again I did and yes, the very same thing happened again. Up he came yet no contact was made. This fish was virtually laughing at me and having much more fun than I was. It was going to be one of those days, I could tell.

Undaunted, I quickly changed the fly for a petite pasty-coloured chironomid imitation on a size 20 hook and cast out once more. The first endeavour produced no effect whatsoever yet I had a gut feeling that the fish was thinking about my fly and the next cast proved this theory to be correct.

A luscious aquatic explosion on the water's surface, a tightening of line all in a flash and the fish was apparently firmly hooked and taking to the air like a mini Polaris missile. However, all was not what it seemed.

An anglers' happiness soon transformed into immediate disappointment as this lovely red-spotted beauty then laughed at me once more as he savagely shook his head, throwing the dressing right back in my face.

"Ah damn it – you were mine" I cursed heavily to myself and sat down on the bank to lick my injured pride. Nonetheless, a few seconds later I created a more optimistic reality for myself as I mused that at least I had managed to get the trout to accept my offering, which in itself was quite an achievement on such a sweltering day. He had also provided me with one of those rare magical moments that are framed in time and space, never to be forgotten. The wonderful sight of such fine fish that are just beyond our reach, just saying 'come and get me', are what makes it all worthwhile. "Good luck to you" I thought to myself "I'll get you another day when the river floods and you are a few ounces fatter".

As the afternoon wore on it became obvious that, like me, the fish were becoming extremely languid and had only one thing in mind which was to go to sleep. The heat was taking its toll on everything that walked, flew, crawled or swam that much was obvious so rather than stress myself into a summer headache I decided to stroll back to the hut and have a nice sit down.

A cheeky grey squirrel, which had been watching me from the safe confines of an old oak, came to check what I was doing. He soon got bored and ran away when he discovered that this over-heated angler was now merely resting his bones on the grass and drinking profusely from a big juice bottle that was emptying rather quicker than I wanted it to. It would have been so easy to down that last pint and a half of orange but I knew that I had to make the drink last as the day was still hot, although it was now around five o clock.

On the far side of the river I noticed a tiny rise, then another only a yard next to it, which helped shake me out of my heat-induced torpor.

It didn't seem that the water was being disturbed by any huge fish yet experience told me not to ignore this offering. As I got into casting rage the fish moved water once more to take what looked like Pale Wateries drifting silently, like pale miniature yachts, from the warm surface film. Hurriedly, I tied on a suitable imitation in size 20 and flicked it two feet in front of the quarry. Oddly, nothing happened therefore I tried again. Could this be a few grayling I thought to myself? The fish rose again yet not to any discernable natural on this occasion so I quickly tied on a red tag. Seconds later the fish gently sipped down my dressing and I had him on.

Although the Silver lady can and does put up a tremendous fight at times they can be fairly lethargic in the hot summer flows yet this was something entirely different.

The line shot through my fingers and I was into something that was more than just eager to shake my fly.

My foot slipped awkwardly on the wet rocks and I nearly fell into the stream as I struggled to get to grips with whatever was thump-thumping manically now at the bottom of the river on the end of my line.

Then all went completely motionless, the fish didn't move an inch and my heart sank as I thought that I'd been wrapped by the fish around some underwater obstacle. However, I needn't have worried for a few moments later the line once again zipped frantically back out into the beck as if some primordial water god had ripped his coat open in anger at the day's oppressive heat.

The fish was now almost visible a foot or so under the surface, shaking its head savagely like an irate terrier with a rat under the peat-stained surface. The next few moments confirmed my belief as I carefully swung the lovely silver bullet into my net. Not a grayling or a brownie however but a beautiful fresh sea trout of about two pounds in weight that looked like it had only been in the watercourse for a matter hours rather than days.

It was a nice surprise and proved as I find is frequently the case that one does not need to go into night time ninja gear skulking about with huge rods, lines, etc to catch sea trout from spate streams.

Although this small success was nice I had not really been convinced that the day would provide me with a great deal of sport. Too much heat and too little water is never a recipe for great angling days on a spate stream so I decided to stay on a little later.

By now the first bats where starting to show around the top of big sycamore and under branches over the far side of the river, hunting indecently like tiny airborne mice for moths and other hapless flying insects. A silently hunting barn owl drifted effortlessly across the meadows like a white ghost and the meadow behind me began to throw up one of those eerie mists which just cover the grass, like the ones we see in old Hammer Horror movies.

It was around nine thirty and the so-called and much-revered 'Evening rise' had not bothered to materialise. I had managed to catch one small grayling of about eight ounces that kindly obliged me with a splashy rise form to throw at yet by and large the majority of fish that I knew were present still appeared to be resting up.

The half moon had by now risen steadily into the heavens and all looked tranquil with the world. Apart from a few distant sheep bleating their late chorus to each other in the surrounding pastures all was quiet, peaceful and very still.

In the failing light actually seeing one's dry fly was now impossible so I exchanged my double strength two and a half pound leader for a one of normal five pounds mono. This may still seem quite light to some yet after being used to having such light tippet on the five pound felt like tow rope. Besides, most of my dry flies go no bigger than size 14s or 12s for special occasions therefore using line any thicker was not an option.

A sudden fluttering smack on the side of the face from a large insect made me realise that a hefty sedge imitation would perhaps be a good starting point on this particular evening. Turning my back to the river so as not to alarm any close feeding fish I used my tiny maglite to rummage around the fly box for a suitable dressing.

As I was searching, several exciting splashes to my rear told me that something was getting hungry in the stream.

I tied on the sedge pattern and although I could not visually see a thing the sense of hearing kicked in nicely. Before long the auditory faculty had taken over and along with what I can only call the sixth sense of intuition I was beginning to see with my mind's eye as if by magic. Hearing and touch were placing my solitary dry sedge into all the right spots and before long the first brownie of around a pound graced my net, then another. Several excellent grayling also nailed the fly and were duly landed.

Around forty minutes later the stream went quiet again and I figured that this must have been some belated Evening rise. However, I wanted more of this exhilarating action so I quickly changed my dressing for a large pale moth on a size 12 hook which is huge by my usual standards.

Although this dressing is exceptionally ostentatious in the daylight it was of course utterly undetectable in this darkness. Even the risen moon, hanging like a piece of giant cheesecake over the oaks, made little difference now as the night was so inky black. Nevertheless, I threw the moth out towards and slightly upstream of a small plop in the middle of the beck and was instantly rewarded with the sensation of a good fish tussling on the end of my line. It turned out to be a decent brown which I swiftly returned to grow larger.

My other senses had taken over from vision and now seemed to be just as effective as the eye. I would even liken this unusual sensation to radar in some ways as one can learn to track an object, in this instance our aquatically-orientated quarry, without the use of normal visual capability.

Yes I concur, the enthusiastic sea trouter swinging his large fancy lures across the stream at night may also experience similar things yet accurately pitching a small dry fly to sounds and feelings is quite another matter entirely.

Although this learned nocturnal gift can never for me personally substitute the thrill of actually seeing that wonderfully dynamic daytime take on the water's surface, it can and does though help us to be greater anglers and people as a whole.

For anyone that wishes to try out the two nocturnal flies mentioned above here are the correct dressings which are simply tied with the bare minimum of effort:

WHITE NIGHT MOTH

Hook: 14-12 up-eyed fine wire.
Silk: white waxed
Body: white rabbit's fur dubbed
Wing: white duck primary feather tied low over body
Hackle: natural white cock about three or four turns tied in front of wing

PAT'S NIGHT SEDGE FLY

Hook: 14-12 up-eyed fine wire.
Silk: bright red waxed
Body: reddish brown cock pheasant tail fibres
Rib: fine gold wire
Wing: speckled brown partridge or grouse feather tied low over body
Hackle: natural ginger game cock wrapped in front of the wing

Both of these patterns can be given a larger appearance by dressing them on longer-shanked hooks, yet this is not an essential. If you make them too large then they will not seem compatible with even five pound leader and you will then have to step up to say seven pounds. The thicker the tippet the easier the quarry can spot it so be warned.

Chapter 15

Using the correct thickness of leader to size of hook is something that is in my experience extremely important.

I have noticed beginners and also those with experience who should know better fishing their flies on the wrong density of leader. This will certainly result in unwanted line breakages.

Trying to get say ordinary five pounds leader mono through a tiny fly's hook eye of size 20 is not a good idea.

Firstly the tiny dressing just looks intrinsically wrong on such bulky line and secondly it hits the water like a hurled brick with bad attitude when it finally lands. Alternatively, the angler who ties a size eight lure hook to lightweight double strength two pound leader material will quite soon discover to his disadvantage that before long it will snap like tinder wood at the first snatch from any little trout. In effect I think that the diameter of your leader should be rather similar to the thickness of your hook or at least as near to it as possible.

Above: a wild brown trout returned to the water.

    Effectively what we want to achieve is perfect balance in our fly and leader combinations and this is one of the chief reasons that I personally use tiny patterns with light lines.
    Furthermore, a nicely balanced set up flips over so well in the air and delivers the imitation exactly like the natural fly with silence and grace. This in turn ensures that the fish is not unduly spooked as so often happens with the clumsy efforts seen by the heavy rod, huge lure, 'Chuck-it-and-chance-it' brigade.
    A good turnover is required with the developed energy travelling down the rod into the fly line then into the leader to end in a nice whip-like flick, which will place the dressing right where we want it in front of the trout's nose.
    I believe that a home-made tapered leader is the best way of achieving this and my set up usually goes as follows. From the end of the fly line I needle knot standard eight

pound mono next to six pound then to standard four pound, then to double strength four and end with double strength two and a half or less. The ready-made braided leader loops that one can buy in the shops are far too heavy for our means herein, and although I have tried them on occasion I cannot recommend them until some thoughtful manufacturer actually starts to make one that is light and insignificant enough to meet our purpose. They may be fine for catching stew pond rainbows but no use at all for the spate streams with delicate presentation being top priority.

The leader set up I have mentioned above will serve to present any dry fly, from the tiniest size 32 caenis right up to a number 14 olive very well indeed. As I have also mentioned before, this type of leader is used with a number three double-taper fly line or even a number two in very low conditions.

The only time I would really consider increasing line size to a number four would be perhaps at night or during persistent heavy floods when the river was high and unsettled. One must remember that as soon as you start increasing the bulk of your fly line you instantly make delicate presentation suffer. So only use the tow ropes above a number three when push comes to shove or if you fish a river wherein distance casting is a main concern for some reason.

Alternatively try out a weight forward taper line if you think for some reason you need extra yards injected to your casting range.

I have fished most of the northern rivers though over the years and have never really had cause to resort to either weight forwards tapers or heavier fly lines in double tapers so that must say something about their actual lack of necessity.

We must remember when dry fly angling that we are supposed to be blending in with the natural rustic surrounding, becoming a part of it all, not bullying it into submission like rabid fools intent on raping the environment just for personal profit.

If we do not show proper reverence towards the river then it certainly will never return the favour. This is a fact of life that many have learned the hard way and some indeed with their very lives. Like does indeed attract like!

A fly should land on the water ever so gently like a descending feather, not like a speeding marble from a school boy's catapult and the correct tippet combo is the first port of call to attain this quest.

It must also be stressed that some so-called dry fly hooks, put out by crafty manufactures wishing to sell their somewhat useless products via manipulation of the more naïve in angling circles, are less than inadequate for the type of delicate angling promoted within this book.

Many have extremely heavy gauge wire and are so thick that they will in fact sink like mini pebbles rather than float as they are supposed to when used with light line. Fair enough, if one only wishes to tease stocked rainbows on still waters then some of these chunky irons are acceptable, so long as they are over-dressed to ensure that they stay afloat like corks in a sink.

Subsequent to numerous years as a fly dressing instructor I have to say that impressing this small reality on novices is perhaps one of the single most important truths they can grasp. For your spate stream dries use as fine a wire hook as you can possibly find.

One of the best used to be the old discontinued Geoffrey Bucknall hooks which were both strong and light at the same time. I and many other dry fly men dearly lamented the passing of this wonderful hook, which accounted for so much great sport.

Saville Ltd of Nottingham however does some excellent dry fly hooks today which are quite good and possess a slightly longer shank. This can of course be advantageous when one desires to create a lengthier fly body even though it adds a little bit more weight to the fly.

I have also always believed that the hook should be so sharp that one can pass in through skin on the radial part of the palm of one's hand with ease and without feeling a thing.

Label me absolutely insane and irresponsible in this matter if you will but in fact when pushed for time by rising fish I have over the seasons habitually stored the odd dressing in the skin in this anatomical position. The left hand is the one to utilise as the rod is held by us right-handers in, yes you've guessed it, the right hand.

After mentioning this rather eccentric and some may say masochistic practice I suppose I should cover myself with a disclaimer of sorts. Subsequently, I cannot however be held medically or legally responsible by any other angler following this somewhat bizarre advice and perhaps inadvertently infecting themselves with some cripplingly toxic river-borne disease and I include it merely out of curiosity value.

So far though I am still here, the hooks have held firmly in the skin of my palm and I have not been forced into seeking my GP's assistance for any form of deadly spate stream hook fever.

Tetanus can be a real problem through in the countryside and especially with any scratches from sharp barbed-wire fences, so do please ensure that you are well up to date with your inoculations.

I had mine last year which were performed by exceptionally friendly nursing staff and all without feeling so much as a pinch in my shoulder. Unhappily, the NHS may be killing off vital services across the land in some towns, for instance my own borough recently lost vital children's A&E etc to another district, yet at least they seem to be good at this one particular practice.

They tell me that I am now covered for ten years therefore I can now leap over those spiky sheep fences, rusty farm gates and blackthorn-surrounded styles as carefree as a gazelle; that is until I accidentally rip the knees out of my waders and have to fork out for another pair. Alas, the British countryside has a great gift for biting back when least we expect it.

Joking apart though, there is no excuse for not protecting yourself these days from nasty things which can be brought home from our more rural areas.

Chapter 16

Seemingly useless angling conditions can very occasionally produce surprisingly good, even hilariously bizarre results on the Spate Rivers of the north for the angler who simply refuses to give up.

One high summer afternoon a number of years ago I made the trip up to the Lune in search of brown trout or even the local sea trout that can be caught therein during the day, so long as one is ultra stealthy whilst going about one's business.

As it happened this time I wasn't alone for my mother, wife Cath and our two dogs had decided that they also wanted a day in the countryside, so who was I to argue.

We arrived on the river at lunch time. There was not a fish to be seen anywhere. The flows ran pitifully slow and the oppressive heat was apparently the only thing that was rising. Still, it was lovely to be there with good company and the skylarks blasting out their timeless merry jingle way up in the blue heavens above.

Although the river was much lower than I would have liked it was not impossible, yet it was certainly below summer level on the gauge.

We sat on the grass and Cath broke out the picnic box and sandwiches, which was an instant hit with all human and canine company present.

Mum was quite pleased to just sit there sunning herself on the grassy bank with the dogs and more than happy to try and spot rising fish, which we knew she would eagerly point out to us if seen. Cath was also looking for any decent rise forms as she was, and still is, an enthusiastic fly angler although unlike me she prefers fishing lakes to the wilder rivers.

Cath and I strolled unhurriedly along the three quarter mile stretch and although it was a glorious day I knew that we were expecting a lot as not one fish was on the fin.

Then unexpectedly I saw three risers on the far side of the river which where clearly taking some sort of fly under the overhanging alders.

"Come on love, let's see if we can get over to them" I said as I drew Cath's attention to the feeding fish. A new vigour had now been injected into our pace and before long we had carefully waded downstream and below these fish over the other side. When we got there we were surprised to look into the peaty waters and see not three risers but a good shoal of at least eight prime Lune browns.

Stooping low I whispered to Cath "just come and look at all these flaming trout – you won't believe it." Like me she was flabbergasted to see such a wonderful assembly of untamed fish and at such close quarters and she replied "wow yeah – incredible".

Thankfully they could not see us. The way that the light was reflecting off the water in front of our position meant that we cast no shadows and the green leafy abundance to our rear ensured perfect camouflage. Moreover, we were in a somewhat elevated position looking down some five or six yards into the waters, which seemed to give us the advantage over this lovely shoal. Nevertheless, we dared not move too hurriedly and kept our voices to a murmur, just in case they got spooky.

As wild brownies go these fellows were not tiddlers either. The smallest was an estimated twelve ounces whereas the best one must have easily been one and three quarters of a pound.

They just sat there resting over the pale gravel bed like spotted ghosts, moving with the odd twitch of their tails, ever so leisurely to sip in the occasional unlucky dun drifting over their lie.

I was itching to get to grips with one of these grand fish. The problem was that they were, as I said earlier, below me and the whole area to both my sides and rear was a jungle of heavy weed growth, overhanging boughs and trailing ivy vines with no feasible way to flick a fly into this relaxed shoal.

It was at first sight an angler's paradise and yet now it seemed to be turning into an angler's worst nightmare. So many marvellous fish just waiting there for the taking yet no way to reach them – what was I to do?

I knew that to rush in like a fool at this stage would have one immediate result and that was to send every fish within sight dashing to the far side of the river, or the security of the nearest submerged bounder. I just couldn't stop watching these trout and with hindsight I must have appeared to any casual observer like a concealed cat scrutinising a mouse before the attack.

Then an idea hit me. To my left only a few yards upstream of my position a larger alder than the rest overhung its gnarled braches across the river more than the rest. With the same feline stealth I very carefully edged to this position and slowly started to walk out over the stream to this new vantage point. Incredibly, the fish were now beginning to move slightly upstream too.

Another unexpected bonus was that a really hefty specimen well over two pounds and a few other smaller ones had joined the party. It now seemed that duns, spinners in the surface film and other insects at a rate of about one in six were being eagerly devoured by some of the shoal members.

Then a thought struck me. No way would I be able to utilise my standard seven foot leaders with all the surrounding weed growth, back-casts were definitely out of the question, so backing warily down the tree again I started to improvise a shortened version of only a couple of feet in length of three pound double strength mono.

With this new mini-leader set up completed I clambered up into position, then waited and watched to get my bearings. It was going to be a matter of in effect just dibbling my dressing into the stream some two to three yards below me and permitting the current to take the fly to the trout; caution was the watch word.

Due to the day's intense heat and plethora of pesky bluebottles etc buzzing relentlessly around my head I was trying not to scratch my self too much. With perspiration threatening to fog up my Polaroid's I figured that every movement I made may have been the one to send these fickle aquatic beauties rushing for cover. This was however not a time to fluff it, I had a rare if unusual opportunity to catch good trout on a seemingly impossible day.

The painful stings of nettles and thistles on my bear arms, gained via my earlier endeavours to get into an effective hunting position, didn't help either yet I mentally brushed such minor annoyances aside as I devoted my self to this current quest.

I was now at last ready to try and lure one of the shoal's inhabitants.

One trout of about a pound was busying itself taking small Medium Olives and the occasional crane fly off the surface, this would be my first target. With a deft twist of the wrist I gently flicked my dressing into the water below which landed too close to the fish for comfort. He backed up and appeared to be slightly alarmed as my daddy long legs dressing passed his neb. Very gently I lifted the fly off the water as soon as it had travelled a safe distance from the shoal.

I was terrified that they would flee into the depths so caution really became the better part of valour and I just waited and watched. It wasn't very comfortable with my legs wrapped precariously around the old alder bough but at least the fish were still unaware of my presence.

The sun cut flickering patterns through the greenery above me onto the water and made dancing shadows on the gravel under the fish. Then with out warning a huge wild brown caused the rest of the pack to move sideward as he pushed his way through the centre of his comrades. I reckoned that this one was easily over the two pound mark and I could see every red spot and golden scale on his flank. He was definitely the boss and the rest of the shoal knew it.

I gently dropped my dry imitation into the languid flow above this fish and he started to move straight towards it. Two seconds later I saw the white inside of his mouth close on my fly and instantly struck. "Blast it" I cursed to my self as the fly came right back at me. Thinking that this would have certainly put the big fish and the rest off I glanced back into the river and to my amazement they were still there, oblivious to my recent failure.

Taking no chances I quickly changed the dressing with slightly fumbling fingers of anticipation for a size 18 black gnat imitation, which was again pinched carefully into the very same taking spot. And low and behold the leviathan moved towards it just like last time. His mouth clamped down on the artificial and I twisted my wrist to tighten the line confident of at last securing a good hook hold. However the gods of the stream were obviously in an especially mischievous mood this particular afternoon and yet again the fly parted company with this fish. This was getting silly now as the whole shoal were as before still there and clearly just enjoying their sunny recline.

The hazardously perched idiot in the tree above them was the only one struggling and even Cath was beginning to wonder what the Dickens I was doing wrong.

"Oh no, did you miss it again Pat" she enquired looking up at me in the tree in a somewhat puzzled voice as I battled to keep any sense of angling dignity, whilst at the same time fighting off a particularly irritating wasp which apparently thought me ears would provide a good nesting spot. "You've not got a harpoon on you have you love" I retorted and she sniggered, not realising that I almost meant what I had said.

This was getting very serious and these last disappointments with the big trout made me want to grass it all the more. It's at times like this that one either says 'sod it' and goes home or persists until the current opportunity fades or the fish is caught. Only the latter choice was though on my mind in this particular instance.

Maybe I had struck too fast I mused to my self or perhaps the fly was simply not what the trout was feeding on, not what appealed to it. Hot days can make fish very fickle and this seemed to be the case at the moment in time yet I couldn't complain because at least they were taking the odd fly. My head was in a total whirl and all manner of possibilities started to filter in and plague me.

Positioning myself once again I slowly dropped the black gnat into the trout's lair. He moved to it as before but this time refused the imitation. I tried once more but still he refused to take it. This was getting rather worrying and I started to think that he may have gone off the feed.

Not to be outdone and with now determination etched on my brow I secured my legs around the tree and exchanged the dressing for a small Greenwell's glory type variant, which I figured would match some of the olives that had been blowing down the waters that lovely hot afternoon.

The imitation fell softly onto the sun – speckled surface film to unite with the naturals which appeared to be increasing a little in volume.

This time the big trout was interested and swung immediately to his side in order to intercept my fly. His mouth again closed around the floating pattern and, forcing my self into extreme focus, I counted one, two, and then 'wham', the fish was well hooked and running like a dolphin into the middle of the stream.

I hung on with my legs for dear life to the tree branch as the trout relentlessly stripped my reel twice down to the backing. I dared not attempt to get out of this treacherous elevated position until the fish tired or at least became more manageable.

I couldn't even raise my midge rod for branches swung dangerously low above me. In effect I had to play the fish with the rod tip almost pointing at the quarry. I knew that as soon as possible it would be essential to get out of the tree to regain control if I was ever to net this hard - fighting Lune trout.

Somehow the fish appeared to be running out of steam possibly thanks to its acrobatic attempts to shed the fly out in the hotter parts of the river. This was good news for me so very carefully I started to scramble my way down the alder's over-swung branch and before long with a sigh of genuine relief I was at the base of the trunk.

I clumsily stumbled into the water below, which was almost chest depth, nearly toppling into the flow but I managed to right myself and keep the rod high into fishing position.

By now Cath had trundled through the high nettles over to pass me the landing net and within the next five minutes we both admired that fabulous red-spotted wild brown trout lying on the grass. It weighed two pounds two ounces.

The rest of the shoal had scattered as I had anticipated at the previous commotion.

Any chance of a repeat performance was now definitely impossible but what a triumph this single lovely fish was on such a balmy day and from such an uncertain as well as completely unorthodox angling position. Minor angling miracles do occasionally ensue if one is in a mind to persist when ordinary common sense dictates otherwise.

As Cath and I forded the river to get back to mum and the dogs we were greeted like heroic soldiers returning from the rigours of battle. They had been watching all the action from their side of the stream and I had apparently provided some fine entertainment, although the dogs seemed more intent of trying to lick the large fish than congratulate me in any other way.

On the way back to the car another angler who had been trying unsuccessfully since early morning passed us by.

Looking at the trout's large tail sticking out of my little creel he enquired with a look of both inquisitiveness and disbelief "My, what a lovely specimen – how the hell did you manage to find one like that on a scorcher like this?"

I smiled and with a wry wink replied "Oh I was just a bit lucky I suppose."

I suppose that another disclaimer may be in order after this particular tale, consequently I have to say that climbing up trees like a frustrated chimpanzee over deep river pools is not something that I can recommend in terms of safety, comfort or genuine angling form. Alternatively though, if one is nimble enough to partake in such passionate schemes then unexpected and worthwhile results can be achieved. Extreme conditions, as I have stated before, frequently demand extreme measures if you are to actually catch any fish.

The dressing for such magical tree-angling, dibbling adventure goes as follows:

TREE-HUGGER'S GLORY

Hook: 18-16 up-eyed fine wire.
Silk: pale yellow waxed
Body: pale yellow silk
Rib: fine gold wire
Wing: Waterhen primary feather tied split and advanced
Hackle: natural red cock

The main object with a dressing such as this one is that it must float well. Don't be afraid to wrap on a few more twists of your hackle around the shank of the hook for if a dibbling fly sinks it may instantly spook your fish, via them being able to see your leader material below the water as it sinks down. Lining fish like this is a main cause of scaring them. I have seen it happen many times.

I do also really prefer up-eyed hooks for my dries if I can get them. They ensure that the first few inches of leader that our fly is tied to points up and away from the water's surface on most occasions. I believe this helps to avoid scaring the fish. I may be wrong but this is just one of those gut feelings which I have stuck by over the years when fishing very fine lines and tiny flies on the becks.

Chapter 17

Very often the angler, who has always relied on wet spider type flies to reap his/her fish from the northern becks, would do well to consider that the dry fly can be equally effective if only given an opportunity to prove its worth.

I speak from a great deal of familiarity with this technique as a previously keen wet fly fisherman at one time my self.

Many of the diminutive spider flies used by wet fly enthusiasts actually travel much higher in the stream's surge that is at first realised.

The invigorated wild little tumbles, dips and runs of a rocky beck force the dressings, which are typically fished three at a time on a leader, high into the current and not many feet below the surface as some angler's mistakenly envisage.

These spiders are also frequently effective, not cast downstream as is customary in many parts, but upstream like a dry fly to the rising fish. As I have stated earlier the downstream method is not selective meaning that a lot of small fish may be inadvertently hooked and it will also on numerous occasions scare the hell out of a good shoal.

Line scare is something the upstream dry devotee is cautious to avoid, whereas the downstream wet fly fisher has little or indeed no control over this matter. Sadly, my experience of watching many perform this latter operation has led me to believe that they are either oblivious to or not caring about the harm this palpable disturbance can do to a feeding shoal.

When delicately using a single upstream wet spider the spectre of line scare can be drastically minimised and this can only be a good thing.

These spiders can in fact be fished almost in the same way as your run of the mill dry fly, e.g. upstream and across to risers. However, fishing them this way has both advantages and disadvantages to consider.

Firstly they are, or should be, extremely sparsely dressed so they are in fact harder to actually see than fully floating dries. This means that takes have to either register at the end of the leader or alternatively the angler must tighten at any surface bulges from the fish in the vicinity of whereabouts he believes his imitation to be. This is not always easy in bad conditions when the surface is broken or the light bad, although I concur that fish may often manage to hook themselves at such times.

Secondly, they can admirably imitate the struggles of the hatching nymphs of various olives in the surface layer or even insects like dying spinners that have become waterlogged. Although I can never advocate their use over the fully dressed dry fly, which gives us the additional elation of that wonderful visual take, I have to agree that fished correctly wet upstream spiders form an efficient and sometimes pleasant method of catching a few fish.

Yes indeed, there are times that these little spiders will come in useful on the wild northern becks. It cannot be reiterated enough that one must dress the bodies of these patterns exceptionally short on the shank though, and employ no more than one and a half to two turns of the hackle. In addition, dubbing should be especially thin so that the underlying body silk colour can shine through. Far too often one will see so-called wet spiders in shops that are hopelessly over laden with podgy bodies, which are obviously aimed more at impressing inexperienced anglers than the finicky old fish themselves.

One will, occasionally find an awkward adversary that is preoccupied with insect life that is in or just below the surface film. Now usually such a fish can eventually be tempted to seize a good dry imitation which purports to be either a natural fly or an attractor pattern such as a Treacle parkin or Red tag.

However, sometimes one does indeed encounter a stubborn fish which refuses all floating artificial offerings and can be seen to ignore the natural flies etc that pass over its neb as well. At such times as this a wet spider pitched gently into the flow, dry fly fashion, may well be the answer if one is impatient to gain some action.

One can also apply a small touch of floatant to the spider's dressing if required, which in fact marks the pattern as some type of amalgam between a wet and a proper dry. Conversely, many times the spider will be more efficient when fished just an inch or so below the surface film as that is perhaps the location that the fish will be expecting to intercept desperate insects rushing up to the surface to hatch out and fly off.

Although I adore creating dries, I have to say that dressing the old North Country spider patterns is also a bona fide delight.

They are so incredibly natural in their appearance and match the insects they imitate so extremely well. One can almost expect them to crawl or fly away as soon as the head is whipped on and the varnish has set. Moreover, they have a fantastic ability to move in the current when tied correctly too. Yes, the old spiders have a genuine following across many parts of the country and this is not surprising. They can occasionally induce awkward fish to take confidently when little else will do the trick.

One thing that I particularly like about them is that they do imitate authentic insects in the stream unlike some of the heavier dressed monstrosities one frequently sees on the end of some casts. I would suggest though that anyone wishing to use the spiders on the northern streams can be sufficiently equipped to do so with no more than a range of around half a dozen types, which will be adequate to match most riverside insects seen.

By and large the spiders are general-type imitations, each of which can mimic a large range of insects rather than any one exact species.

For instance let's take the Waterhen bloa which is an admirable old country dressing that can in springtime imitate the hatching nymph of the Large Dark Olive better than most. In the same instance it will catch fish that want to feast on hatching Blue Winged Olive nymphs in summer too.

All in all it will be effective when most of the drabber coloured olives are struggling to achieve adulthood and can be of course dressed in a variety of sizes. The same can be said for many other spider patterns too, although there are perhaps a few exceptions to this unwritten riverside statute.

That purple-bodied killer known to most river anglers, the Snipe and purple, due to its body colouring is very successful at periods when flies like the Purple Dun or Iron Blue are on the water but may understandably be less effective when the hatches subside. Its success comes from the splendid way in which it imitates the body colouring of such naturals although many anglers who rely on it implicitly all season will not even be aware of this fact. Its big brother is of course my own Purple Dun dry fly discussed earlier in the book.

The same may be said for the partridge series of flies, which exhibit various body colours. Some of these replicate certain drowned spinners, stoneflies and sedges awfully well. However, the angler will perhaps never know or at least be certain exactly why his Partridge and red or orange worked so well on that particular summer's evening when largely undetected Sherry Spinners were drifting silently in or below the surface film or why he stopped catching when the surreptitious hatch petered out.

The hidden secrets of the stream are perhaps then known less well to the wet fly anglers than they are to the dry fly advocate who can actually see his pattern drifting amongst the naturals that surround it on the surface of the beck. As they say, 'seeing is believing' and it forms a great part of the understanding of the angler towards the life which abounds on the stream. If you don't actually observe what is happening with your fly amongst the naturals then you can only have faith and little else about what is really going on beneath the watery flows. This fact alone gives the dry fly fisher a distinct advantage over his wet fly angling counterpart.

I often feel that the mystery of not knowing what is actually occurring under the surface is a great part of the attraction to some anglers. Perhaps this particular motivation provides them with a distinct magnetism for the wet fly in the same way that the fervent ledger fisherman waits in anticipation for that electrifying bite to register on his quiver tip when an outsized unseen roach takes his sweet corn.

Although throughout this book I have sought to promote the wondrous art of the dry fly on wild becks mainly because this is my utmost passion, I would never attempt to decry any other legal method of angling for we are all different at heart. And that that is indeed the way it should be.

One man's poison is another man's remedy and what a lacklustre old world it would be if we were all the same. Long live the angels of diversity!

Chapter 18

One fascinating tale of how unexpected results can occur when using an upstream wet spider comes to mind, which I will share next with the reader.

For an early April morning it was quite a pleasantly still sort of day. Hardly a breath of air ruffled the lines of sycamores along the riverbanks and all felt well with the world.

It was not quite frosty. Cool dawn dew had coated the grassy meadow, whilst the distant mountains surrounding the Lune valley were shrouded in an eerie white fog. My waders crunched solidly amongst the white pebbles as I made my way towards the river's edge.

A startled oystercatcher near to my feet noisily 'peep peeped' its complaint at me as it exploded across the river like a black and white projectile, making me jump unexpectedly.

These striking birds along with distressed pheasants and anxious partridges in the pastures must create more heart attacks than the NHS could ever imagine, for unsuspecting anglers who inadvertently step into their territory. And as soon as the angler forgets about them they seem to get under one's feet. 'Sod's law' was never displayed more capably than by the uncomfortable way they can make one almost collapse with instant fright when least expected.

I had managed to take a brace of brownies around a pound and a half on a dry LDO, which had risen well behind a huge boulder out in the middle of the stream. Yet now it seemed that the hatch was over and the fish had returned to the safekeeping of the river bed for the day.

This was rather unusual as they frequently got tucked into the tasty dun hatches until well after midday, yet perhaps I was just being a little impatient. The early season fish can sometimes give us great sport for periods of around three to four hours and usually around late morning to the start of the afternoon. Call it the 'Lunch-time rise' if you will but that is very often when the action gets underway in the cold days of the early trout season on the becks.

However, during the March and April LDO hatches there is certainly a feeling of anxiety in the air. What if the hatch fails to materialise, what if the flies are too sparse, and what if one is too late getting down to the river.

All these old doubts and excuses can and do set like stone into the lone angler's mind, when the fish are not that eager to look up towards the surface to find their lunch.

In fact I probably would be quite affluent if, as a keen dry fly fisher, I had been given a ten pound note for every season that I had privately sworn to 'not bother' visiting the stream so early the following spring due to LDO hatches being either too emaciated or totally nonexistent.

It has to be said that near frostbitten fingers, headaches, colds and other assorted lovelies, due to savage weather conditions, can have a most depleting and disheartening effect at times on the new season angler. Nevertheless, as the highly addictive dry fly can be a form of masochistic enchantment the old charisma starts to pull one back to the seemingly inhospitable banks of the feral northern becks as soon as the trout season starts anew.

When the LDO hatches are really sweet and the trout are on the fin in abundance there is no finer place on earth than the wind-swept streams of Lancashire, Cumbria and Yorkshire.

Cold and damp are soon forgotten when the nomadic olive sailboats come drifting past our position only to be brutally gulped down by a large, ravenous brownie.

When the adrenaline kicks in we are transformed from shivering wretched bipeds to stealthy hunting machines with a single purpose – to tempt that wonderful fish, which is just out there waiting for our imitation in the cold bleak waters of the beck. Then the solitary angler is close to paradise and never more alive!

This particular April morning I had an odd feeling of expectancy, the sort that tells one that something rather diverse is about to happen and my instincts proved me right.

I crossed the river to the far side as the previous sport with the brownies had stagnated. They just ceased to rise as swiftly as they had started. This is often the case in spring.

I should however have remained on the side where my earlier fish had been taken, for as soon as I got onto dry land I heard a hefty splash behind me and then another. Something was obviously on the feed and I was travelling the wrong way to find out what it was. "Right – here we go again" I mused to myself.

Turning to wade back over the ankle-deep shallows of the stream in order to get into a suitable position, the fish once again drew my attention and it was not a small one judging by the huge bulge it had created in the water. A few minutes later I was standing directly opposite its rising position waiting for it to show. Although I had not yet seen sight of it, I knew mentally that it was holding in a deep pool some ten feet deep. I waited and waited as the minutes ticked by and nothing farther occurred. Frustration was threatening to attack me like a sledgehammer, so rather then feed the ogres of impatience I decided to change my fly.

As I had previously observed several stoneflies on the wing of various sizes during the morning, I looked into my box and picked out a Partridge and orange wet spider. Experience has taught me that this dressing is excellent when these insects are about.

Again I waited, then the fish moved water once more yet annoyingly it never gave me a proper sight of itself. Nevertheless, I now had its exact location marked well in my mind so out went my fly just inches in front of where I knew it would be.

The dressing swung enticingly past the place where the fish was lying and travelled a few yards downstream. Not to be deterred I swiftly lifted my line off the water once again and punched the spider a little farther upstream in front of where he was.

My eyes strained hard to focus on the area where the fly had sunk just below the surface and I knew that it was only just swinging a matter of inches below the water past this huge trout. Any amount of drag at this phase would have frightened the fish so I was doubly careful to make certain that enough slack remained in the line to keep things looking as natural as possible.

This time fate jumped in for me and moments later another bugle at the end of my line caused me to tighten instinctively. He was on and apparently well hooked.

The fish burrowed deep and fast and, trying hard to catch my breath, I suddenly realised that this was no ordinary Lune trout.

Another angler looking on had seen that this fish had been keeping me busy for almost twenty minutes. As he walked down the bank and stood by my side, the fish once more went towards the peaty depths.

"What you into there mate – looks a good 'en" exclaimed the other fisherman curiously, as he glanced up at the acute bend in my fly rod. Not wanting to seem impolite yet at the same time not wanting to take my concentration off the vital job in hand I replied. "I don't know but I don't think it's a brownie – good sea trout perhaps."

I couldn't put too much pressure on the fish, which incredibly still hadn't shown itself, as I was only fishing with my usual light leader strength and the fly itself was only a size 14.

After several more minutes that quarry tired and both my new found friend and I looked at each other in amazement as not a sea trout but a shiny young salmon slid obediently into my waiting net. It weighed just less than six pounds, not a giant in Salmo salar terms, but it was certainly a fight to remember on light trout gear and a cheeky little North Country wet fly.

Now whether the fly had actually been floating when the fish took it I will never be certain. Yet if it had grabbed the pattern on the top then I could have claimed the salmon to be almost 'dry fly caught'. As it was I was quite pleased to have had this nice bit of sport with the so-called 'King of fish' on whatever one wants to call the given technique of that particular day. This unusual experience also goes to show that one does not always require huge rods and large flashy lumps of spinning metal or plastic attached to twenty pound breaking strength mono to hook and grass salmon.

The heroic little fly held very well in the scissors of my fish and although it had taken me quite some time, I eventually beat the fish. It was later returned to the chilly stream to fight another day and learn how to dodge the excesses of the 'genuine' salmon angling brigade.

Chapter 19

By the time that the lovely month of May has arrived on the northern becks, several flies have for the most part disappeared from the surface.

The Large Dark Olive, which kept the angler so busy in March and April, has usually gone. The same can be said for the March brown (Rhithrogena haarupi), a big brassy fly that is either usually ignored by a lot of fish or taken with savage gusto.

When this species is capturing the attention of the trout one usually has no doubt at all about it for it's quite a violent affair with water splashing about all over the place. It's as if fish know that they have to nail the fly hard and fast due to its bulk, although I often feel that when they have filled their stomachs they may resort to harassing flies - just for the fun of it.

The best thing about the March brown is that in the colder spring months it can provide a little extra sport for the angler after the LDO hatches have finished off around afternoon.

It almost seems to give the trout a substantial dessert, which of course is also a dividend for any keen fisherman hardy enough to stay on late and brave the cool early season winds that frequently blast down some of the more exposed spate streams.

Another good thing about the March brown is that it grants us the opportunity to have an excellent view of our fly even at extreme ranges. It's so big that there can be no mistake when the fish hits our imitation, although at times smaller fish may fail to connect to it, again due to its large size.

When this happens a trout will attack the dressing with immense verve and yet somehow not actually manage to get the item into its mouth, causing an exhilarating surface splash but with the fly shooting right out of its jaws, like one of those tame pool dolphins playing about with a beach ball. I do think nonetheless that in some ways this can be an advantage to the angler for smaller fish are frequently unable to take the big dressing down, whilst the real thumpers easily can. This can be most frustrating yet the angler who persists will habitually sooner rather than later connect with a good quality fish.

From the point of view of the ultra light-line enthusiast one disadvantage of using large dressings instantly springs to mind.

Recalling what I stated earlier about the correct leader thickness to size of pattern, one must seriously consider that big fly dressings usually require large hooks and therefore much thicker leaders.

One way around this predicament can be to tie large fly imitations on a small hook but with the various components of the fly oversized, such as bigger than usual wings and longer hackles etc. We do though have another small problem when we try to achieve this. Huge looking dressings on light leaders frequently create line twist which makes the whole leader swizzle itself into a terrible bird's nest screw up, if one is not careful.

I would suggest that at times like this one must to some extent increase the leader thickness and constantly check for line twist. It's not always an easy thing to do but at least it gives one the capacity to match the hatch of a larger insect and stay in the game. Furthermore, dispensing with any wings on a large March brown pattern will help to ensure that line twist is kept to a minimum. Any decrease in air resistance can only work to one's advantage at such times. Also, because we will dress this fly with a large hackle, less turns are required than usual to keep it afloat which again results in less coiling of the line as it travels through the air. Do though of course use as thick a leader as you can get away with, yet keep in mind the fact that fish will not take your fly if they get spooky about your line.

If you are faced with a substantially flooded river and the fish are heavily into the March browns then you should be able to really step up the leader strength.

If on the other hand you are on a thin, clear brook and they are hitting the big flies then you will have to be much more cautious. This may of course seem like stating the obvious but it has to be said.

Here is a typical March brown dressing to try out at these times:

PAT'S MARCH BROWN NO. 1

Hook: 14-10 fine wire, long shank.
Silk: pale yellow waxed
Body: brown rabbit or seal fur dubbed
Rib: yellow tying thread
Tail: natural brown cock
Wing (optional): thin slips of hen pheasant primary, tied to lie back over body
Hackle: natural brown cock
Additional hackle: one twist of speckled partridge tied in front of the other hackle

This fly is either tied very fully then and fished on quite a substantial leader if conditions allow or alternatively it is tied in a finer style, without the wings, and fished on thinner leader. The ultimate decision as to how it should be created and utilised must rest with the individual angler alone.

I would though suggest that no angler should ever visit the river in March or April without having at least a few various types of this dressing in the fly box. Getting caught without one when the trout are hard into this insect species is so incredibly annoying and wholly avoidable.

Hatches of the March brown are frequently very scrubby affairs with just three or four insects coming down the stream at any given time. Although on occasion they do come off in great profusion.

I have found that the drizzly days are perhaps favoured mostly by this insect and this may be due to the fact that damp weather aids their transition from hatching nymph to adult fly. Squally showers are no deterrent to this insect. On warmer days they may struggle to get through the stickier and flatter surface calm. Of course I could be mistaken about this but it seems to make good sense after observing such events first hand myself.

The trout get ample opportunity to scrutinise this big fly on slower deep pools and can sometimes be seen head-butting March browns and trying to drown them, like playful cats with butterflies. This type of intense activity is fascinating to watch and almost as exciting as actually catching the fish at times. One minute a fly is floating sedately past your position and then 'wham,' it's pulled roughly under the waves to only pop right back up again like a manic children's plastic toy duck in a bathtub.

This sort of rascally trout activity is quite hilarious, although not I would imagine for the hapless insects themselves that only desire to fly off into the wild blue yonder.

Trout that want to feed on fast shallow runs are forced into a make or break course of action. They have to make up their minds hastily as to whether or not they want to take the natural March brown before its gone past them in the rapid flow. This gives the prudent angler as excellent chance to utilise his dressing and know that it will either be totally ignored or savagely gulped down by the trout, usually without any of the annoying messing about as can habitually occur on the slower reaches of the beck.

Now whether it's just coincidence or not, I don't know, but I do find that the larger rivers get more extensive hatches of the March brown. On rivers like the Lune, especially the upper reaches, hatches can be rather dramatic events with dozens of March browns littering the surface. However, these hectic episodes don't seem to last very long unlike some of the hatches of smaller olives.

Most anglers can be forgiven for not realising that several flies look extremely similar to the March brown, and to be honest this is not of primary interest to us within the scope of this particular book. However, for the sake of clarity one may wish to be aware of the following.

The Large Brook Dun (Ecdyonurus torrentis) is very hard to distinguish from the March brown yet it can sometimes be a little larger. It has a preference for smaller becks and tends to hatch from early spring up until May, although it can be seen later well into the summer depending on weather conditions. The same patterns that catch fish feeding on the March brown will quite easily suffice for this species too. I recall that a friend and I once spent several days seeking to identify both of these species from each other on the high reaches of the Lune in the end I think we gave up and decided to just catch fish instead.

To confuse matters even further we also have the Late march brown (Ecdyonurus venosus) which again is similar to the other two species. I can only reiterate that the angler should not worry too much if any of these species are encountered as the general March brown pattern given in this book will be sufficient to match all these flies.

All in all, it is a magical period when even the local acrobatic sand or house martins along with dippers and tail-bobbing wagtails join in with their aquatic associates to enjoy the early feast.

The wet fly fisher may also do well at the same time now as the dry fly enthusiast and it would be rare for him to fail in his attempts to secure a few trout when the March brown is hatching out in profusion. A March brown spider pattern can be a real killing pattern, yet if you want to use one do undoubtedly always ensure that your leader is up to the job and strong enough for takes can be fairly ferocious. A one pound trout can easily shatter standard three pound line travelling downstream like a carrot at these times, consequently if you must fish wet do please be warned.

Chapter 20

When May does finally arrive all manner of things start to take to the wing.

On dull days we get the Iron Blue Dun (Baetis niger) putting in a welcome appearance, although appearance may be too strong a word to use herein. This is mainly because this dark coloured little fly is quite difficult to spot in certain lights. However, it does stand out well on the surface when the light is shining on the water and causing it to create a more distinctively petite silhouette. The Iron blue's apparent insignificance is in stark contrast to its effectiveness as an excellent source of food for the fish.

Yes, when a bright pool makes one's eyes squint painfully in defence then is the time to see the drab Iron blues, which then stand out like miniature black corks above the surface film. However, they seem to disappear like magic when we try to observe them against dark, choppy waters. Then, only the gentle splashes of feeding trout give away their clandestine presence. When this occurs many anglers can be forgiven for thinking that fish are feeding on nymphs instead of the almost undetectable dry adult dun. Perhaps this is why some rush to put up a cast of wet flies at these times.

Above: big grayling of Lancashire's wonderful River Hodder.

The fish do seem to love the taste of this fly and one can almost be guaranteed sport when it's on the wing. As the body of the insect is only some five millimetres in length I would suggest that small dressing are the order of the day. I have often seen anglers fishing with huge meat hooks of size 10 and more and having the audacity to call them Iron blues. Even four adult flies of this species glued together would have quite a hard job to fill the size of such a bulky hook. Aim to use small hooks for this one.

IRON BLUE DUN

Hook: 18-22 fine wire, up eyed
Silk: dark claret fine
Body: stripped peacock herl
Tail: Iron Blue Dun cock
Wing (optional): grey slips from a starling's primary feather, split and advanced
Hackle: Iron Blue Dun cock

This pattern can also be tied without wings for a more delicate effect, yet the wings do give it such a naturalistic appearance on the water. Both male and female duns are such beautiful little flies and look so well-groomed with their inky body colouration. Although I have to say that on closer examination the colour is nearer to dark olive brown with some specimens becoming a very dark green.

Catching and studying a given fly is a sensible thing to do for the keen naturalistic angler, for an insect appearing to be one colour at long range will often as not be a series of contradictory shades in the hand. The legs, eyes, abdomen, wings etc of a fly will be various colours yet when you see the insect out there in the stream you just get an overall impression and this may be deceptive. Look and learn is the lesson herein.

Interestingly, the Iron blue's male spinner is dubbed with a feminine title, i.e. the Jenny spinner. This is an extremely handsome, petite fly with a jet black thorax and a frosty white body. The female spinner of this insect is called the Little Claret Spinner and has a much darker claret-brown body but seems to prove more popular with the fish than the fancier male spinner. Although these elusive spinners may not be of much interest to the dry fly angler, due to the fact that they often go undetected below the surface, they show up throughout the whole day.

In May we start to also see the Medium Olive Dun (Baetis vernus) coming into its own. They have a similar sized body to the Iron blues, although sometimes a little larger, and they are not quite as dark. I have always associated them with milder days and that is when they seem to hatch out best. One need not be too fussy either about the dressing to match this little fellow, so long as it is tied delicately.

MEDIUM OLIVE DUN

Hook: 18-20 fine wire, up eyed
Silk: cream waxed
Body: pale cream rabbit's fur thinly dubbed
Rib: olive thread
Tail: pale olive cock
Wing: snipe primary feather, split and advanced
Hackle: blue dun cock

The Medium Olive Spinner is usually reddish brown in body colouration; ergo any ordinary Pheasant tail spinner dressing will suffice to match it. This is a well known pattern so I won't labour the point herein.

A particular favourite of mine at this time of year is the Olive Upright (Rhithrogena semicolorata) which looks very like a Large Dark Olive although it is a smidgen bigger. Hatches of this insect are often best when the water is not too warm. It seems to dislike intense heat and can be seen at any time throughout the day, although tea time is when I usually encounter this fly. As with the Iron blue the fish do like the taste of it and it is taken with aggression and flamboyance by most trout.

When the Olive Upright is drifting down the beck things certainly do get exhilarating. I have good reasons to like the Olive Upright.

OLIVE UPRIGHT

Hook: 16-14 fine wire, up eyed
Silk: pale yellow waxed
Body: natural mole fur dubbed
Rib: yellow tying thread
Tail: blue dun cock
Wing: grey slips from a waterhen's primary feather, split and advanced
Hackle: blue dun cock

On one memorable May afternoon on the beautiful River Doe near Ingleton in Yorkshire I was facing a hatch of this insect. However, not that many were trundling down the water yet every one I spotted never in fact managed to get into the air. The fish had other ideas.

The trout were so intent on nailing them that they appeared to be almost lining up, like expectant passengers at a bus stop, to take turns for a shot at the title of who could eat the most flies in the shortest time.

I wasn't complaining though. Even one or two of my fumbled attempts to drop the fly accurately into the curved horseshoe surge of the pool in front of an overhanging willow, where the trout were lying, never seemed to bother them in the least. They just kept rising without a care in the world making me feel like the Invisible man. More than once I had cursed myself for ineptly clonking the end of the fly line across their rising positions, yet again and again they were so preoccupied with the still rather meagre Olive Upright hatches that they forgave my clumsy errors.

The same cannot be said for many occasions when various duns are hatching whereabouts a trout will instantly take offence at the first sign of a ham-fisted angler's drastic fish – scaring mistakes.

The Olive Upright dressing is also a cracking pattern to have on one's leader when the fish have been especially awkward all afternoon and the light begins to fade.

On many electrifying occasions I have taken lovely trout with this fly that have hit it hard indeed and without any previous warning or messing about. I would though strongly urge anyone who has been fishing very light line earlier in the day to step up to higher strength leader prior to tying on the Olive upright, before night comes in. Takes are savage affairs and the trout have no intentions of letting this dressing pass them by once you have them in the mood to tango. Sea trout will nail it at times as well. Be warned!

Anglers call the Olive Upright's Spinner the Yellow Upright Spinner due to its attractive wing colouration. It seems to like dancing about at evening time under overhanging branches that crown the river. Poetry in motion it is too when observed making its climbing and swooping displays in unison with many others.

Yellow May Duns (Heptagenia sulphurea) are a pretty sight on our rivers and trout are peculiar in the way they deal with them. I have seen naturals taken at times but on other occasions they just let them pass safely by.

Perhaps they have a distasteful favour of hot English mustard as the colour suggests – I've never eaten one yet so who knows? Alternatively, when other flies are scarce possibly they are better than nothing so the trout have a little nibble to keep them going until something more acceptable turns up. They never do seem to come down in any great magnitude so this in itself could be the reason for their occasional lack of fish appeal. Very often trout need to get in the mood for a fly, either our artificial or the natural insect, before taking it well.

I usually carry an odd imitation of this insect but to be quite frank it's never in my top five of choices as a cannot – do-without killer pattern.

The last fish I caught on a Yellow May Dun artificial was actually foul-hooked very lightly in the dorsal fin and fought so frantically to get away that it almost had me thinking it was a small salmon. Such hooking is quite uncommon in dry fly fishing and indicated that the trout was only nosing the dressing rather than taking it properly.

Perhaps the playful trout use these vivid flies more for head-butting entertainment or sporting practice, like a kitten with a ball of wool, than as an essential dietary food item.

Although the fly's usefulness to the angler may be to some extent debatable, the following dressing will doubtless give some entertainment on the right occasion; although the trout may have more fun with it than the fisherman. Be warned!

DRY YELLOW MAY

Hook: 16-14 fine wire, up eyed
Silk: pale yellow waxed
Body: pale yellow dyed hare's fur or similar
Rib: olive tying thread
Tail: cream dun cock
Wing: slips from a waterhen's primary feather, split and advanced
Hackle: pale yellow dun cock

Another insect well worth mentioning in the merry month has to be the Hawthorn fly (Bibio marci) or St. Mark's Fly as it is sometimes called due to the fact that hatches often occur from this saint's day, 25th April, whose feast day probably in turn links back to much older Greek/Roman Pagan celebrations.

As the name implies this somewhat gangling black insect is regularly found around the flowering Hawthorn tree or smaller bushes that line the river banks in May and impart such a lovely aroma to the stream when in blossom.

There can really be no finer place on earth to be than sitting on a green hillside close to the babbling stream when the May tree, Faerie tree or Quickthorn, as it is sometimes colloquially know is sending its heavenly bouquet across the lush green meadows.

This fragrance can be quite intoxicating and some say that the tree can make birds that overindulge on the berries (haws) become quite drunk. Herbalists do use it to regulate the heart, so maybe there is some truth in this claim. Personally, I can vouch for its use as a lovely country wine which is velvety smooth – so long as you don't mind spending the time gathering all those white blossoms.

The Hawthorn fly's dark body contrasts blatantly with the almost incandescent waxen blooms of the tree when the insects are feeding in abundance. The long dangling legs of this gawky fly are a dead give away when it's zooming around the aromatic flower heads and what the angler really wants is to find a sunny day with a good stiff breeze. This is because they are such maladroit insects that they frequently end up getting themselves blown onto the river where they drown. Of course the trout, as expert opportunists of the highest order, take first-class advantage of such events and mop them up with great relish.

Then again, perhaps some of the ill-fated insects that hit the water in similar fashion to later-day kamikaze pilots have, like the alleged locally boozed up blackbird etc, managed to get themselves a little too inebriated with the overpowering nectar of the May tree. I suppose that unless one can get themselves reincarnated as such an insect one will never really know the truth of the matter. Wind or wine – who ever can say for certain?

The Hawthorn fly's larvae feed mainly on the roots of grasses and such like, marking it as a terrestrially-based insect. They are occasionally also unwanted cereal pests as well as feeding on putrefying organic material and are regularly found in compost heaps. On a more positive note they do seem to have an important part to play in pollinating fruit trees and bushes. The males are easily distinguished as they have enormous bulging eyes giving them a larger head in contrast with the females.

In our northern parts I have seen the major hatches of Hawthorns during mid May on the River Lune, especially throughout periods of warm weather when the barometer's glass is rising. They do seem to favour hatching when the day is pleasant as opposed to the dull damp days preferred by some other flies.

Here is a simple dressing for matching the Hawthorn fly:

DRY HAWTHORN FLY

Hook: 14 - 16 fine wire, up-eyed
Silk: black
Body: black seal fur dubbed
Thorax: black seal fur dubbed a little fatter than the body
Legs: knotted fibres (about four will suffice) from any black feather
Wing: a stubby slip of white duck feather tied short over the body
Hackle: natural black cock in front of wing, The knots in the legs are I feel quite important in helping the fly to look natural, although I do appreciate they are a little tricky to add

It's best to use a small dubbing needle when creating legs. I have tried out contraptions aimed at making leg tying easier but personally I don't care for them. Furthermore, I find that the knotted legs aid in the floatation abilities of the dressing. As with most dry fly methods seek out your fish first visually; don't just cast blindly into open water like a hopeful lure angler.
When you find a good riser cast your Hawthorn fly to it and before long, so long as your casting is accurate enough, you will reap a just reward.

Chapter 21

Similar to the Hawthorn fly yet smaller in size and without quite such long gangly legs is the Black gnat (Bibio johannis), an insect treasured by both still water and river fishers alike.

However, the Black gnat's angling designation can cover numerously comparable insects of the same genus, which hatch at various times throughout the season. I recall being on the Lune several seasons back and having a chat with a gent who had previously attended one of my evening fly dressing courses. I mentioned that Black gnats were on the stream that morning and without delay he politely informed me that there were numerous species of this particular fly within the surrounding area. He was a qualified entomologist so who was I to argue.

For angling purposes though, which of course is the objective within this book, we need not be over concerned about largely inconsequential differences in various families of insects and I dare say that the fish are not usually that pernickety either. However commendable it may be to take up the complete study of entomology, for practical fly fishing purposes it will not as a rule result in more fish in your net. However, the fly angler should have a good general working knowledge of the type of insect species that inhabit his preferred watercourse for if he has not then failure will often be his riverside companion.

Like the Hawthorn fly the Black gnat can also find that it often gets itself unstuck on breezy days, frequently ending up in the water much to the delight of the waiting fish. When walking upstream to seek out risers it may seem obvious but try and keep an eye peeled for flowering hawthorn bushes overhanging the stream. If you are lucky enough you may find fish rising below these places, all lined up nicely waiting for the unfortunate insects to fall in.

This dressing is as good as most to match the Black gnat and has served me well over the years.

DRY BLACK GNAT

Hook: 14 - 16 fine wire, up-eyed
Silk: black
Body: black seal fur dubbed
Tag (optional): small twist of flat silver tinsel
Wing: a small bunch of white hair cropped short to run no more than half way down the body
Hackle: Natural black cock in front of the wing, the silver tag is at times an added bonus and helps to create the illusion of trapped air in the dressing

In May time one or two stoneflies hatch out but to be honest I have never paid them any great amount of attention as a dry fly angler.

However, the Large Stone Fly, a designation which covers several different but similar species, can be occasionally appealing to the fish when it returns to the river's surface to lay eggs. Then a dressing which is large enough may take a trout or two. It however has to be remembered that this insect can have a body length alone of around twenty four millimetres so its imitation would call for outsized hooks and strong enough leader to handle such a hefty pattern.

As I have stated before, it's no use trying to fish enormous lure size flies on thin double strength leaders so do consider this if you must spend a morning trying to secure trout with imitations so large.

You may instead opt to try and imitate the Yellow sally, another popular stonefly, which is conspicuous by its yellowish green colouring. This fly is smaller at around ten millimetres in body length and therefore can be imitated on less substantial hooks than the latter.

There are also numerous other stonefly species, which can be encountered at various locations and periods throughout the season. Willow flies, February reds, Early

Browns etc may on the odd occasion have their respective part to play. I do not though wish to labour this particular entomological clique as I have never been a fan of it. I can only reiterate that in my experience it is never as popular with our quarry as the olives and other flies mentioned so far. Or is that just the dry fly angler in me speaking out of turn? You decide!

Nevertheless, it would be wrong of me to dismiss this species entirely out of hand from the fly box, so the following dressing tied in various sizes may just save you a blank day.

DRY STONEFLY

Hook: 14 - 20 fine wire, up-eyed
Silk: grey waxed
Body: brown rabbit fur dubbed
Wing: any drab grey or brown feather rolled tight and tied flat over the body
Hackle: natural blue dun, grey or brown cock in front of the wing. Make sure that you use a short-fibred hackle herein as the natural insect is slender and long so a bushy hackle will not look correct

And still looking at what to expect around the month of May, one insect in particular springs to mind.

The Small Spurwing (Centroptilum luteolum) is a lovely little olive which certainly does get the trout keyed up at times.

I have seen good hatches of this species on the Lune yet it is not always so enthusiastic to show on the Hodder or alternatively perhaps I was just not there at the right time. Small spurwings seem to prefer shallow stony runs as opposed to the deeper pools. I recall that the hatches on the Lune suffered some years ago when the salmon men moved into a local fly fishing club and persuaded the Environment Agency to permit them to make alterations to the river.

Salmon numbers were sadly given preference over the natural trout habitat and short- term deepening of pools and creation of groynes etc resulted in greatly reduced hatches of this and other olives. Lovely ancient shallow trouty runs were replaced with very deep, canal-like stretches which may have doubtlessly held more salmon but at what cost to both the native trout and all the insects that they depended on. Salmon anglers with access to huge earth-moving vehicles are something which makes me incredibly uneasy, and I do speak from experience in this matter.

I and a few others called it authoritarian – approved ecological vandalism, whilst others saw it as a necessary evil to increase holding pools for greatly-prized salmon and sea trout stocks. Many of the more blinkered salmon fanatics actually forget that apart from sometimes ruining the native environment, which Mother Nature has created in her wisdom over eons, when the river decides it can and does very quickly silt up such disgusting man-made ravines. I do seriously wonder though about the Environment Agency, that should know better, granting permission for such crimes against nature at times.

At first glance the Small spurwing is very similar to several other species, yet look a little closer and you will see that it lives up to its name with a small spur being seen on its hind wing. Another peculiarity is that they used to be called the 'Little Sky Blue', which is rather quaint. Again though this nickname is rather accurate as in certain lights it can appear to have a bluish tinge, particularly when seen on bright days with a little sun.

Some writers have suggested that they are no more attractive to fish than any other olive yet I politely beg to differ.

The Small spurwing is relished by trout and any serious angler would be advised to carry a suitable imitation during the months of May and June – just in case.

Try this one yourself when you see them on the water.

SMALL SPURWING

Hook: 18 – 20 fine wire, up-eyed
Silk: pale yellow waxed
Tail: blue dun cock hackle
Body: grey goose herl or substitute
Rib: pale yellow tying thread
Wing: a pale grey starling split and advanced
Hackle: natural pale blue dun cock

The body given above is suitable for imitating the male, which is slightly darker than the female. For the female body one should aim to use a paler shade of goose or substitute although any pale fibres from a duck or whatever will be fine. Alternatively, dub either the male or female body with pale mole fur or rabbit on light yellow thread. Being overtly fussy is not compulsory as with many such dressings. A broad impression of the insect, giving special attention to shade, size and shape, is what we are looking for and not a precise reproduction which can never in point of fact ever be achieved.

I recollect once reading an especially level-headed article by some well-known sea trout connoisseur; I think it was the late Hugh Falkus, wherein he stated that the fly pattern should aspire to be an "impression" of the thing which the quarry is feeding on and not an exact imitation.

Although he was referring to some such huge fish imitation the advice was quite sound.
We can never hope to achieve total cloning of a natural with our dressings and if we did then we would not in fact be imitating the flies on the water at all. No, if we wish to do that then in all reality we merely become bait anglers and may as well throw lobworms or maggots at the trout. Based on this latter point, I have a distinct abhorrence for many of the so-called flies which we see today in fly fishing literature. The great use of synthetic materials like plastic and various

shiny and glittery materials, as opposed to the traditional fur and feather, is a real turn off and I feel largely misses the whole point.

Yes, admittedly many of the Stateside-orientated plastic creations we now see on sale in fly angling catalogues may be very lifelike to us yet they fail to achieve that wonderful illusionary impressionism I mention above. They are so real looking that in the water they appear very often to just be exactly what they are – hard lifeless lumps of plastic and glue. Alternatively, a few skinny wisps of hackle from an old coot wing will and does give that magical impression and appearance of life that we should be attempting to generate in our fly dressings.

I will hold up my hand and state though that I was once seduced by the realism fly dressing brigade. I created a few wet and dry patterns that looked so lifelike that they made most females in our family jump at the sight of them.

However, the fish thought differently and absolutely detested the things, refusing to snatch them at each cast. As soon as a proper old traditional went on the fish played the game again. I had at the time proudly displayed these 'real' insect patterns in my fly box and was met with the expected 'Cor blimeys' and 'Wows' from exceptionally impressed fellow anglers, yet what good is realism when it fails to achieve results on the stream?

Very often we use the same natural materials found on the banks of the rivers to create our flies. The fish expect to see these materials and consequently are not alarmed by them. On the other hand, inorganic plastic latex and other more simulated substances look and smell different and are in fact alien to the quarry. It's a bit like someone replacing our cornflakes in a morning with a version that looked exactly the same yet was something quite extraterrestrial in makeup.

These synthetic masterpieces may of course also impress stocked rainbows at times but there again, in my experience; I reckon that even these fish prefer a good old impression of a food item instead of such artificial things.

Call me opinionated if you will over this issue but I include it in good faith.

I have to say that the only artificial material I have ever really taken to has been SLF (Synthetic living fibre) and poly yarn. SLF is though a little shinier than its natural counterparts and again poly yarn must be used rather sparingly; nevertheless, given the Desert Island choice the normal equivalent wins hands down in my book.

Yes I am prejudiced in this instance, give me the natural fur and feather anytime over those beautiful and oh so realistic yet lifeless works of art that are so much-loved nowadays by angling magazines seeking to astound their frequently inexperienced readerships.

Now perhaps it is some kind of strange coincidence but in my own experience the Mayfly (Ephemera danica) is in fact quite uncommon on our northern streams. The ones that I have come across have only been solitary specimens and of little interest to the trout, save for stirring up a few excited parr. However, on occasion this outsized insect will create a bit of a fuss and fire up the adult fish up. It does though never seem to be seen in the enormous numbers expected by our southern fly angling brethren.

The few northern Mayflies I have observed have been in areas heavily surrounded by trees and not in barren open waters.

I reiterate again that matching such a big fly with a body length of sometimes almost twenty millimetres calls for a large hook to be incorporated and thus thicker leaders. Although the temptation to resort to such things when a couple of mayflies are spotted may be quite understandable, one might also be more prudent to stick to the lighter leaders I advocate and stay vigilant for signs of rising fish taking smaller flies in abundance.

Although one may never in fact require it on the wild becks of the north, I shall give a simple dressing which will suffice for all practical purposes.

DRY MAYFLY

Hook: 10 long shank (larger if you can manage to cast it on your light leader)
Silk: white waxed
Tail: blue dun cock hackle
Body: cream fur off a rabbit, hare or similar
Rib: thick black thread
Wing (optional): grey duck split and advanced
Hackle: natural pale blue dun cock

Omit the wing if you get into trouble with line twist when trying to use thinnish leaders. Sometimes leaving out the wings can be a good idea with big dressings because it will not only allow you to fish better, via avoiding dreaded leader twist, but it may also assist you to emulate the more fragile spinner of a fly species rather than the dun.

A fly which is awfully similar to the Small spurwing is the Pale Evening Dun (Procloeon pseudorufulum).

This little fellow also looks very like a Pale Watery yet it is, as the name indicates, paler and slightly larger than the other two. I have seen good hatches of this fly on warm evenings in the slower pools of the Hodder when both trout and grayling tuck into the feast. Body shade is almost creamy white in some specimens. After other duns have dwindled then is the time to remember the Pale Evening Dun, which also occasionally attracts the attention of sea trout. Incidentally, sea trout certainly do feed in fresh water at times and anyone who thinks otherwise is wholly mistaken. I mention this point as some anglers appear to be under the misapprehension that sea trout, like salmon, don't feed subsequent to their re-entry into rivers.

Here's a little pattern that will match the Pale Evening Dun quite well.

PALE EVENING DUN

Hook: 16-18
Silk: white waxed
Tail: grizzle cock hackle
Body: creamy white fur off a rabbit, hare or similar
Rib: pale yellow thread
Wing: starling primary split and advanced
Hackle: natural cream dun or grizzle cock

    The spinner of this fly frequently falls later in the evening after dark so unless one is able to fish late they may never be encountered. Alternatively, you may find a few around if you get to the water very early on in the morning around the more lethargic stretches of the beck. Big sluggish bends in pools are the sort of place you may discover them close to shore rocks and that is where the fish may also be. In appearance they are a most fragile and nice-looking creature with a straw coloured body.
    Never forget to pack a few various colours of midge imitations in May either. Huge swarms of Chironomidae can occur at most times in the season yet mild days are perhaps best. And when fish are really interested in midges then nothing else will do.
    I clearly remember one afternoon on the River Lune when I was faced with a shoal of several ravenous fish which seemed to be taking something extremely small on or in the surface film.
    I saw very little coming down the stream in way of tiny duns or spinners and my previous attempts had failed to secure one of these nice fish. However, looking down at my feet I noticed a series of very minute midges both hatching specimens and adults drifting past and around where I was actually standing in only inches of water.
    Immediately, I exchanged the olive I had on my tippet for a tiny hatching midge imitation and on the third cast a

good trout bulged at my fly. Feeling somewhat elated, I cast again and this times the pattern was gently sucked under the surface and I connected with the quarry. Minutes later the fish stopped thrashing in the stream and slid into my net.

Try this dressing at such times and tie it in a variety of body colours.

HATCHING MIDGE

Hook: 18 – 24 fine wire, up-eyed
Silk: fine waxed colour to match the same as the body
Body: stripped peacock herl, tied with equal spaces to permit the body colouration to shine through
Thorax: a tiny ball of dark mole fur
Wing buds: a tiny stub of white duck behind the hackle
Hackle: natural pale blue dun cock very short in fibre and thinly

The idea with such midge dressings is to keep them fine and delicate. In effect they are fished exactly where the trout want them, which is right smack bang in the surface film. If they float too high in the water they are likely to be refused so don't overdress them. If takes are not easy to achieve then permit them to fish almost wet spider style, just below the surface film.

Tighten your line gently but positively at any hint of movement at the end of the leader or any sign of a protuberance near where you figure the fly to be.

Fish them on very light double strength tippets and don't strike hard or else you may break on first contact. Indeed, at times heavy strikes are counterproductive when fishing the midge and if you get into the knack you will find that, so long as the line is not unduly slack, fish frequently hook themselves. If the fly seems to sink overly fast and goes down like a pebble then grease the leader up a little.

Favourite midge body colours on the becks are perhaps olive, black, red, white and cream. These will suffice in the majority of situations, yet if you want to play it safe then get to work at the fly vice and have fun creating as many coloured midges as you can envisage in different sizes.

Another tip is that applying a slight dab of fly tying varnish over the body can help with durability and give your dressing a little shine. Don't over do it though or else you may substantially add to the heaviness of your midge and make it sink rather than drift gracefully in the surface.

Presentation in this type of fishing is the key to success for no matter how wonderful your dressing actually looks it will catch less than nothing if you just chuck it out and hope for the best. Place your concentration right into the heart of that dressing at all times; even if you cannot actually see it on the surface see it with your mind's eye and expect the fish to take it any moment.

Looking and expecting the take to come is in itself an art form, a strange skill which can be increased over many seasons with eager practice. One could almost liken it to the devoted fortune teller looking attentively into the crystal ball – waiting for the swirling mist to clear so as to see signs, visions and entries of past present and future.

The fly fisher must also possess the very same centre of attention and expectation.

Again, the hunting cat, or even cheetah if one wishes to muse in exotic terms, displays the same aptitude for single-minded anticipation which we must strive to attain on the wild stream.

Above: the deadly dry Black gnat.

Unhappily for them, many aspirant spate-stream anglers will never quite achieve this invocation of the latent hunting instinct yet a rare few will – if they only seek it out and bring it to the frontal parts of their minds.

One particularly well-accepted yet erroneous maxim exhibits this type of wrong thinking so well, which displays exactly why many will never achieve to reach the solitary hunter's indispensable state of mind.

'You need patience to be a fisherman.' Most folk will have heard this saying and nothing could be further from the truth when applied to the spate stream fisher. It's in fact almost an insult.

If you are seeking to be patient then you are probably better off sticking to sleeping all weekend in a little tent with a flask of tomato soup, whilst leisurely waiting for a fat carp or tench to carry off your boilie. Either that or take up train-spotting, bridge playing, watching TV soccer or something else not requiring the mandatory employment of mans' dormant hunting instincts, which once eons ago meant the difference between life and death.

Patience will not in any way shape or form cut it on the wild becks when your fly is drifting past a hungry brown trout that is about to devour your olive dun. No, the call for patience will never do when the dry fly angler is at any moment anticipating that big fish to turn another inch and greedily nail his dry fly.

The patient 'sit-down and lie back' angler must by virtue be a passive soul and indeed wait for his quarry to come to him, either by means of float or ledger methods etc. Alternatively, the dry fly beck angler must hunt out his fish, he must go to them, and become a part of their ways, lifestyle and surroundings if he truly wishes to gain success. He must be proactive, extremely vigilant and decidedly travel-orientated.

If the mobile angler is not catching fish then he needs to step up his game plan and think harder about just what is happening, or indeed not happening on the watercourse. Unlike the serene sit-down freshwater angler he cannot afford the extravagance of just going to sleep and setting up a bite alarm. He must watch the stream like a hawk and be aware of everything that is occurring around him.

He is in effect everything that the patient course angler is not. Naturally there are exceptions to this tenet, such as the eager trotting enthusiast who needs to stay in touch with his/her bobbing float as it zips past a feeding shoal of roach etc. However, I include it as an example of the mind-set which is by and large essential for success on the wild becks.

If the call for patience has any place for the dry fly fisher then it must be during periods of trout inactivity. Nevertheless, at these times one can always have a pleasant amble upstream and seek out more obliging fish that are on the fin.

Yes without doubt, patience may be a virtue for some yet it can also be a hindrance to the dry fly man who must become a part of the quarry's habitat and ways if he really wants to perfect his art as far as he can.

Chapter 22

June brings with it the promise of great fishing for the dry fly angler who has access to wild becks.

All sorts of insects are now flittering onto the increasingly warmer waters and so long as drought is not a problem it can sometimes be the best time on the season. Most of the species encountered in May can still be about yet other species of fly now join them.

One of my all time favourite upwinged flies, the Pale Watery Dun (Baetis bioculatus) has by now started hatching in profusion. Any angler that has foolishly forgotten to include quite accurate dressings to match this little fellow may as well stay at home for such is its enormous attraction to the fish.

It hatches during all sorts of weather conditions too, but actually seems to prefer those mildly buoyant days when the birds sing loudly, the air tastes so fresh and everything seems at ease with the world.

It is a rare day that never sees at least one hatch of Pale Watery Duns and they are a mainstay of trout interest. I've never eaten one myself but the fish do love them.

Just watch carefully as petite flotillas of these delightful flies come leisurely down the stream and one can almost guarantee that they will be eagerly taken by trout. It's rarely a vicious affair though with just nice positive rise forms, ensuring that the fish get the fly with minimum exertion.

The Pale Watery is not a large insect at around five millimetres in body length so the fish have no effort in actually gulping them down off the surface.

It must be stated that the Medium Olive can be quite similar yet it is often a little larger. To confuse matters further the Small Dark Olive is also rather comparable to these two flies. The Pale Watery does though tend to typically have a paler body colouration as the name suggests.

As I have said before the direct reproduction of the natural is not what we are after, so do not despair if you have difficulty identifying these particular upwinged flies accurately. An impression is the key to success.

I have discovered that when matching the Pale Watery, the combination of using both yellow and grey in the body dressing is especially valuable. It appears to me that by winding both these colours together on the body we grab the trout's attention exceptionally well.

Why this is so I cannot be certain. It may be that rather than just using a solid colour like olive or grey in the body-making material we again aid in the impressionistic qualities to fool the fish, via this method. An analogy may be in the mode that impressionist artists use all manner of colours in their art in order to create the illusion of light and shade, rather than the older solid realistic work by the old school of traditionalism.

Who knows; perhaps our quarry is more artistically-inspired than we ever give it acknowledgment for.

There again, the body colour split attraction may be due to the fact the various duns display a different shade on their dorsum (top) and venter or under part of the abdomen. Unless though we can ever reincarnate into an actual trout these are simply theories and nothing more. Whatever the real reason it matters not one iota to me for I know that it works, and that is the proof of the pudding.

I know for a fact that when I get the body colour just right on my Pale Watery dressings it really does make all the difference to success. This is not just a random belief but a reality gleaned from many years of experimenting and recording catch rates on the rivers.

Tails and hackles are important too yet if I was pushed I think that I would say correct body shade in our dressings is more crucial to success than hackle tone. I cannot prove this though apart from the fact that it works like I expect it to when I have the colour precise in the body. Moreover at certain times fish will oddly take dressings that exhibit hackles which are not quite in accordance with the naturals yet also have an accurate body suggestion. Therefore I am inclined to believe that the trout often pay considerably more attention to the actual body of an insect then any other part of its anatomy.

This is all relatively feasible when we comprehend that the abdomen and thorax of the insect contains more essential nutrients and vitamins than the rest of the fly. Perhaps greater experience and maturity will change my opinion on this issue but until that day I have to follow this gut instinct, dictated by the intensifying ways of the river and its watery inhabitants.

Although I have already given a dressing to match this dun earlier in the book do please try out this next alternative pattern when the Pale Watery start to show in profusion. It can be a real 'no- can- do- without' killer.

PAT'S PALE WATERY

Hook: 18 – 22 fine wire, up-eyed
Tail: pale blue dun cock
Silk: fine waxed pale yellow
Body: any slender strip of pale grey herl off a duck or goose, alternately dub on pale grey fur
Butt: a twist or two of yellow thread at the base of the tail
Rib: fine yellow thread
Wing: pale grey starling or even sparrow primary tied split and advanced
Hackle: natural pale blue dun cock

The spinner of this fly is called the Pale Watery Spinner or sometimes the Golden Spinner, a title which more properly applies to the female of the species due to her lovely body colouration. The male is distinguished from her by his large yellow eyes and darker thorax. They certainly form a pretty sight meandering down the stream in numbers on calm summer evenings.

Without wishing to get excessively complex concerning the entomological side of angling within this particular book, I will give the following spinner dressing which can be utilised for the latter species and varied accordingly to match others with relevant colour changes, et al.

GENERAL SPINNER PATTERN

Hook: 14 – 22 fine wire, up-eyed
Tail: pale blue dun cock
Silk: fine waxed pale yellow
Body: pale creamiest yellow hare's mask dubbed
Rib: fine white thread
Wing & hackle: natural pale blue dun cock which is tied split and spent laterally into two bunches and in effect also forms a wing

Now, one can use any suitable body colour for the mainstay of spinners to be expected on the angler's preferred streams. You can also vary the wing/tail shades too. The prime concern with spinner dressings is that they should appear to rest just above or in the surface film. If they don't then they just become dun imitations. Do remember that on most occasions one cannot actually make out the natural spinners coming down the stream due to their low, spent position in the water. Consequently, you should not really be able to see your artificial any easier.

Dress them sensitively too for the real insects are tantalizing creatures even in the larger sizes, much more so than their heavier dun counterparts

Along with damselflies and dragonflies I often think that the creators of the old flower fairy paintings (e.g. C.M.

Barker etc) may possibly have been influenced by the short-lived, ephemeral beauty of the multi-coloured spinners that grace our becks. The way in which so much loveliness can be discovered within these uncultivated places is of course a true and long-lasting credit to wondrous Mother Nature herself.

Many of the older, long-established spinner dressings such as a Pheasant Tail were also tied with appropriate fragility yet perhaps at times with an ordinary wrapped around hackle as in olive imitations. These are quite capable artificials and will catch fish well but do remember to use the minimum turns of hackle so that they rest low in the water keeping the above comments regarding a sensitive touch in mind.

Above: a happy angler, Kyle Regan, with a brace of Yorkshire trout.

So-called spinner patterns in many fishing tackle shops sit like wine corks and appear quite alien on the water because of this and don't tempt many fish that are essentially feeding on natural spinners.

Many is the angler who has however claimed success for his heavy-weight spinner dressing when in fact he has done little more than secure a trout that thought it was devouring a late dun.

Fly fools a fish or Fly fools a foolish man? At times the Difference is closer than we at first like to imagine! Still, if the angler is happy with the result then what more can be said – perhaps the end really does justify the means on occasion.

By and large spinners of the various species will be more effective in the early morning or late evenings. This is of course simply a generalisation and variations of hatch periods do of course occur.

For example, a good spate after a dry spell when the river has been on its bones can get spinners out in force quicker than one may imagine. Subsequently, always be on the look out for them around your feet in the water. Another sign of them is when fish are obviously rising fervently to something on the surface that you just cannot make out. Rise forms appear as if they are taking a good-sized insect yet one that is so far annoyingly impossible to distinguish.

If you are certain that you are not being faced with fish just taking minuscule terrestrials, midges or tiny caenis etc and that they are not swirling under the surface at hatching nymphs or even fry then do suspect spinner activity.

Of course the size of spinner taking their attention will dictate the type, or I should say intensity, of rise form. Large spinners will elicit hefty swells and bulges, whilst small spinners will usually create gentle sipping rises from the trout.

As usual, make use of your eyes and ears to get as much data into your head about what is happening all around you. The hearing faculty will perhaps be more significant to you when fishing with spinner dressings for as we have already observed it is usually undertaken when light levels are not as good in the full light of day.

It's quite surprising too how one comes to learn the subtle differences between the sounds of fish taking say Golden Spinners as opposed to the larger Sherry Spinners. Again, the hefty crashes of trout hitting the pertinent flies give one's hearing as much information about what size of pattern to tie on as the eyes do earlier in the day. As the day changes so must we.

June also brings in the Angler's or Fisherman's curse the Caenis, which we have already discussed briefly earlier in this book.

The name itself is rather misleading in my eyes for although this fly can drive an inexperienced angler to distraction it can also be another angler's joy.

Trout and grayling do become wholly preoccupied with caenis on occasion to the exclusion to everything else. The angler that dismisses this species is quite unwise for the sport it provides is unusual, exciting and quite sophisticated.

As when fishing the midge, the fisherman seeking to imitate this tiny fly must fish especially fine. Leaders must be delicate enough to handle the dressing which can be as small as size 32. At times the tippet needs to be no more than say one and a half pound double strength leader material to fool the fish. If the water's surface is calm and unruffled then this is preferred, yet a ripple may permit us to increase to around two pounds with the same material.

Trout and also grayling mopping up on caenis like to pack tightly together and sometimes one can mistakenly think that only one fish is being covered when casting rather than three or four in a group, apparently working industriously as a team.

Dorsal fins, nebs and tails gently breaking the surface film are good signs of caenis feeders. Woe betides the unprepared angler who comes along excitedly with some ordinary shop bought caenis of say size 18 or above. The fish will by and large totally ignore his efforts and cause him to curse the flies that he cannot match. Yet let a man seek out the same fish with light leaders, stealth and minute flies relevant to the task and sport can be vigorous.

Accurate casting is essential though as the fish at these periods want the pattern just inches in front of their noses. A fly that falls a foot to their side may typically be ignored for although they can eat hundreds of these tiny insects per sitting they do not seem to wish to expend energy by swimming about all over the beck. This is understandable for when on caenis trout have no need to zoom about as the flies come down with such abundance that the fish only have to virtually hold their positions and open their mouths in order to gain a veritable feast.

Striking is largely not required as the fish suck in the caenis flies like a proverbial vacuum cleaner, and very often they hook themselves well. Do not get into the habit though of allowing a fish to gorge on the fly as we have a duty to never allow any fish to get itself hooked farther back in the throat than we would like. If this ever happens then a small pair of artery forceps, available from any good tackle shop, will easily help with swift extraction. A course fisherman's ordinary plastic disgorger, in the finer sizes as utilised by match anglers, is also a very good tool to aid with hook removal. The latter of course only really applies if one is set to return the fish quickly to the stream; otherwise the customary swift blow to the head with the priest is the first operation if one requires the quarry for traditional table purposes.

The fun really starts though when we have to play them and such minuscule hooks can easily pull out, even when we are being as careful as we possibly can. Aim to connect with a taker by gently lifting into him and do not apply too much pressure, which can be fatal. Let the rod do the work and stay calm when the trout grabs your caenis imitation. Even if every other fish gets off at least you will have the satisfaction of knowing that you are indeed matching the hatch, fooling the fish and catching more than the thoughtless Herbert upriver who is incredibly expecting these cunning fish to grab a hold of his size 10 meat hook caenis wonder fly.

Now, to add insult to injury at times our friend fishing with his gigantic dressing will unbelievably catch a fish. This I feel may be due to the possibility that the fish may mistake a large white dressing for a group of caenis clustered en masse. Nevertheless, in my experience the solitary fly is the one which does the damage when the fish are preoccupied with these diddy chaps. It's such an exciting time too.

At times it is difficult to know whether the fish are on duns or spinners of the caenis genus and this is due to the fact that the transposition from one stage to the next occurs extremely swiftly. The angler need not really be too fussy though as a general caenis imitation will usually be adequate. The duns are a little darker than the creamy spinners and the fish like both although with perhaps a slight preference to the paler spinners.

The fish can be rather forgiving for some reason when on the caenis and ignore most angling mistakes, which would normally scare the pants off them. I would say that the main drawbacks though from the angler's point of view are possible headaches due to extreme concentration levels and the flies themselves, which can creep and crawl around your eyes, face hands and neck.

Still, such inconsequential annoyances are usually tolerable in exchange for the brilliant sport brought to us by the curse.

Although I have given one dressing earlier in this book to match the caenis do please also try this one.

DRY CAENIS

Hook: 24 -32
Silk: micro fine white
Body: creamy white thread
Tail: two or three cream cock hackle fibres
Hackle: creamy cock very short in fibre and minimum of turns

The mere fact that this fly dressing is so diminutive permits it to float well. Because of this I reiterate that only one or two twists of the hackle are required as any more will just make it appear too bulky.
The nymphs of caenis live in mud and are silt crawlers. The next dressing should be also fished dry or at least right in the surface film to imitate the hatching nymph. This can be useful if you are faced with a particularly awkward group of fish that refuse your tiny dry adult pattern. In fact fish this pattern just like you would a midge dressing as we discussed earlier.

DRY CAENIS HATCHING NYMPH

Hook: 24 -22
Silk: micro fine white
Body: creamy white finely dubbed fur off a hare's mask or similar tied to taper thicker towards the head end
Thorax: a dubbed ball of darker hare's fur
Tail: two or three short fibres from a cream cock hackle

This dressing floats very well again due to its tiny dimensions and the manner in which the body/thorax material traps air. Larger nymphs though, say tied on hooks bigger than 20, would most likely sink which in this instance defeats the object.

Chapter 23

By the time that July rolls in so does the Small Dark Olive (Baetis scambus), which appropriately used to be called the July Dun.

This little upwinged fly though is rather uncommon on some of the more northerly streams and seems to be found in greater quantities in places like Wales and the south eastern regions of Britain. Furthermore, if it is encountered on the northern becks then any of the smaller olive dressings discussed previously will easily suffice to match it.

However for any angler who requires to have a dressing with a name then this next pattern will serve the purpose.

SMALL DARK OLIVE DUN

Hook: 18 – 22 fine wired up eyed
Silk: fine pale yellow
Body: olive dyed goose herl or similar
Rib: brown thread
Tail: grey cock hackle
Wing: small slips of starling tied split
Hackle: dark blue dun or dark olive cock hackle

This frequently hot and waterless month is famous for one other species of fly in particular, the Blue Winged Olive (BWO).

It hatches in great profusion all over the country and the spate streams of the north are no exception.

However, a number of angling authors have mistakenly suggested that the BWO hatches exclusively in the late evening yet nothing could be farther from the true. Given a nice bit of fresh water in the beck following a spate and we see great hatches of this species throughout the day.

Yes, when the keen salmon and sea trout anglers stroll down to cast their flashy lures into the murky peat-stained waters of a flooded spate stream, then is often the most excellent time to expect the BWO to make a welcome appearance.

Thankfully too the BWO is rather easy to identify with its laid back smoky blue-grey wings, three tails and olive-tinted body which can though darken in specimens found later in the season to a brownish hue. Once properly recognised something about this dun just shouts out its identity. The way it sits proudly on the water with its wings held so far back and its entire noble countenance tells one precisely what it is.

The smaller male dun is recognised from the female BWO not only by size but also by his big red pop-eyes which appear almost comical. The fish are not often very particular about whether to devour males or females yet on rare occasions they do seem to be a little more selective, preferring one sex over the other. And there is no doubt when the larger females come down the beck for they really do appear quite a bit heftier than their prospective husbands.

It's such an obliging fly too. The BWO continues hatching from the middle of June through the trout season and sometimes, when the weather is kind, right into the customary autumn grayling period. At the risk of reiteration I must say that the main advantage we have up north is that, unlike our southern chalk stream counterparts, we get frequent flooding which certainly does encourage BWOs to hatch at different periods of the day. They do seem fond of highly oxygenated runs. Therefore if the river is low and the day is difficult seek them out behind the somewhat faster tails and heads of pools rather than deep stretches.

I recall one hot lunch time rise in early July on the Lune. The sun-scorched rocks surrounding the river which were usually grey looked white. It was indeed quite hot and I was thankful that I'd left my fishing jacket in the car.

The stream was a lovely shade of port wine and falling steadily, judging by the tide line of twigs and other debris from the previous night's downpour. I had arrived on the river later than expected yet I wasn't too worried as the waters had obviously been coming clearer by the hour and I figured that the best was yet to come.

I was in my element because only one other angler had beaten me to the bank and he actually looked like he was heading for home.

"Are you off then" I said to this fisherman as I passed him on the shingle. He had a huge salmon fly rod in his right hand and looked rather dejected.

"Yes, I've had enough – there's nowt doing and I have been flogging away for three or four hours with a tube fly" he replied, looking despondently down toward his feet. "It's a total waste of time" he continued.

The poor chap was only interested in catching migratory fish and seemed wholly oblivious to the good brown trout that I could see rising constantly out in the stream behind him as I glanced over his shoulder.

"You trouting then mate?" he enquired as I gently blew my BWO dressing to remove any excess floatant. "Yep – I'll be giving it a try" I responded as my concentration waned from his question to the second rising fish, only ten yards out in the beck. They looked like very nice trout too.

As this gent glumly plodded away from me in the direction of the car park, I instantly took up position in only six inches of water behind a large waist high rock and started to flick out the artificial towards the feeding fish.

The salmon angler was only some twenty yards past me when on the third cast the first brownie dragged my BWO violently under the flickering ripple and took off like a manic torpedo, making my reel scream.

Several acrobatic minutes later the one and a half pounder was heading for my waiting net. The chap had stopped in his tracks after hearing the trout's splashes and my reel singing and strolled back to watch the battle.

"By the hell that didn't take you long – what you got on" he enquired in a somewhat animated voice. "Just a dry BWO – that's what they're taking off the top" I replied.

There was no great mystery in it yet the man seemed amazed. He had spent hours throwing a large black and orange brass tube fly in the hope of catching a big salmon and failed. Alternatively, I had arrived moments ago, analysed the feeding habits of the species present and instantly given the quarry exactly what they wanted. He went home with no fish and this thought in his mind whilst I fished on with confidence that more trout would reach my waiting landing net.

I was not disappointed and the earlier success was repeated. I managed to grass seven trout that afternoon on the BWO. I kept a few for the table and released the rest. The best was two and a half pounds and the smallest weighed in at one and a quarter pounds.

Furthermore, half a dozen overenthusiastic lure anglers presently rolled up on the river with their huge double-handed rods, obviously drawn in by the nice spate. They of course expected to catch lots of salmon and sea trout, but although several good ones rolled in the deeper pools none were taken.

I just quietly continued to seek out the lusty risers, some of which were definitely sea trout, and had an exquisite afternoon with grand sport. One could though almost smell the growing pessimism as the day grew on into early evening for these unproductive salmon men.

There was however an exception. One exasperated salmon angler decided that enough was enough and, after anxiously seeing me catch the fifth excellent trout, he decided to change his tactics. He understandably wanted some of the real action.

Nevertheless, although his heart may have been in the right place and his willingness to seek the feeding fish commendable, he was not fated to be lucky.

This however was perhaps due to the fact that he somehow expected these BWO-obsessed browns to grab hold of his wet team of three. The trout though had no interest whatsoever in his size 10 Peter Ross, Teal blue and silver and hefty Invicta that he persisted to throw at them.

I admired his readiness to at least try and catch a trout yet, as is frequently the case, this angler just didn't get it. The penny hadn't dropped at all.

The small dry BWO was the only thing that had caught fish, because that was what they were eating.

The rest of the anglers went home in self-induced frustration including this doubly-confused salmon turn coat. If only he had bothered to ask me or used his eyes he may have discovered exactly what the river and its inhabitants were trying to tell him. If only he had thought sincerely about tempting trout with proper imitations to match naturals rather than hedging his bets and lobbing those big unproductive lake patterns at these erudite fish. If only he had shown the wild browns the due esteem they deserved, he may then have put on an effective pattern done the business and taken a fish.

Similar experiences have occurred for me on many occasions and I really should be happy that most anglers who visit the northern spate becks do appear to be wholly salmon-orientated and unaware of the wonderful trout fishing available therein. I cannot though accept such masochistic behaviour for myself as I do like to catch fish yet for many it almost seems to be obligatory. Walking away from eagerly rising trout on a beautiful wild beck is abject torture and the stuff of nightmares, at least in my view. Should not fly fishermen seek to catch feeding fish with a fly – rather than go home dejected because some large species such as salmon that may or may not be in the river system refuses to grab their chunks of metal? Perhaps I am being small-minded but it all seems quite illogical to me.

Two choices exist on the spate streams; either one may opt to plug away at possibly absent or unseen migratory giants with a lure and risk 90% frustration, due to the habitual failure that goes with that game. Alternatively, one can learn the secret ways of the beck's feeding inhabitants and enjoy regular wonderful sport along with increased awareness of one's situation.

Although I do on occasion fish for the silver monsters just for a change, I can by and large see no contest in the above choices. Nevertheless, the world and indeed life in general would be most tedious if we were all the same.

It just seems that when the BWO visits the northern spate streams so too does the heavily geared up lure anglers, en masse.

Thankfully though, the trout can be rather forgiving when the stream is flooded and a shiny series of Mepps, Toby lures and Flying condoms etc are being pitched at the habitually uncooperative salmon. Trout expect to see all manner of debris coming at them during floods such as tree branches, dead sheep etc so a few metallic spinners perhaps seem insignificant then. This is however not the case when the waters ebb away.

Mercifully, when the stream is lower the lure-bashing brigade that often queues up on the banks like clockwork soldiers stay at home. Hatches of the BWO still occur at these times albeit not in such good numbers as when a deluge brings the waters up. Then the angler must be more careful in his fly presentation and movements and respect the trout which has once again resorted to its suspicious habits.

Try this dressing for BWO hatches as it can be most effective.

THE BLUE WINGED OLIVE ADVANTAGE FLY

Hook: 18 – 14 fine wired up eyed
Silk: pale orange or dark red later in the season
Body: finely dubbed mole fur so that the tying thread shows through
Tail: grey cock hackle
Wing: small slips of coot or waterhen primary feather tied to slope back a little over the body, almost like lake, wet fly style
Hackle: dark blue dun or dark olive cock hackle tied in front of wings

Again, the dualistic mix in body colouration helps to achieve that magical glow of illusion which appeals to the fish so well. I sometimes also like to create a tiny orange/red head, which helps to match the eyes of the male dun very nicely.

Above: the charming River Yarrow in Lancashire.

Although the BWO is largely olive or brownish in body colouration the spinner of the species sports a sherry red or even at times brighter red body. The Sherry Spinner is certainly a welcome insect for both trout and angler alike. Dressings to match either the dun or the spinner do seem to be more effective if they employ a little red or orange in their make up. On occasion one may be seeking to imitate a dun and catch a fish that is feeding on spinner or vice versa. This is not surprising when we consider that both stages of the insect may be on the water at the same time.

Spent spinners falling well upstream can get washed a long way down and although we might not always realise it the fish may be taking both at the same period. Consequently, it is prudent to add a touch of colour as mentioned above to the dun as well as the spinner dressings you create to match the BWO.

Customary Sherry Spinner dressings and the ubiquitous Pheasant Tail will also suffice for the spinner hatches. And another old pattern, the Orange Quill, is effective when either duns or spinners come down. This latter dressing was I believe originally tied with a hot orange dyed, stripped condor quill. However, I have found peacock herl dyed the same colour to be excellent for this particular fly.

Although we have discussed spinners previously in this book, another tying method which is effective does spring to mind for their makeup.

By using the tips of cock hackles a suitably light and delicate wing can be furnished which sits in the surface film very well. However, if you do utilise this method ensure that the tips are whipped in laterally just like the dead spinner's wings do in the water and not sticking up in the air as with duns. This helps to create the necessary buoyancy too, which in turn makes the spinner artificial look so acceptable to the fish in the water. Use very little turns of the hackle also as too much along with the hackle point wings will kill the delicate effect stone dead.

Try out this next hackle-point winged dressing, which is based loosely on the Sherry Spinner.

HACKLE-POINT SPINNER

Hook: 18 – 14 fine wired up eyed
Silk: pale orange waxed
Body: pheasant tail fibres
Rib: orange thread
Tail: pale grey cock hackle
Thorax: dark rabbit or hare's fur
Wing: blue dun hackle points tied spent
Hackle: blue dun cock hackle tied very sparingly

Of course, by varying the colours in the body, hackle etc and by using different sized hooks all manner of spinners can be replicated. The main thing is to try and record what is on your particular stretch of river instead of just blindly accepting third-hand information printed out be some distinguished expert who may never have even cast a line on your stream.

There can be no proper substitute for first-hand personal experience and anyone who thinks otherwise is either trying to be manipulative, via some hidden agenda, or a complete and utter fool. Just because some widely accepted expert stated many years ago that say a certain spinner must be dressed with such a coloured hackle etc does not mean that it will be correct for your purpose. The insects on your little beck may admittedly be the same species, yet their appearance can be vastly different to another on a wider river only ten miles away.

Keeping an open yet vigilant mind then is all part of the waterside art and the only genuine way ahead for the naturalistic fly angler.

Another very useful insect that crops up around this time is the Large Green Dun (Ecdyonurus insignis). Evening is a fine time to watch out for its emergence after a warm day.

With its big mottled wings, in appearance this fly is a bit like the March brown yet much paler with a decidedly greenish hue as the name suggests. It's a large fly too with a body around twelve millimetres in length. Once the fly is identified it is quite easy to recognise again and it certainly knows how to get the trout into violent activity, although hatches are usually sporadic affairs with only a few duns coming down at any one time.

Because this dun is large it poses the problem once again of delicate presentation. However, as hatches of this fly are often later in the day and into the darkness one can step up leader thickness as deemed appropriate. It is usually one of my prime choices for later on in the evening and as soon as the light realty starts to fade then out pops the meagre hatches of Large Green Duns.

The very similar Autumn Dun (Ecdyonurus dispar) can have comparable effect on the fish yet I have not noticed it in quite the same numbers as the former on our northern streams. Either way though as July slips into August these two flies can make all the difference to catch rates if the angler is prepared to stay on a little later into the evening. Sadly, the sort of hectic sport encouraged by these big duns never seems to last very long, so do be aware of the occasional need to switch to them if the naturals suddenly show up.

This next dressing, which I have given quite a pretentious yet at times very accurate title, will suffice for either of the above mentioned flies.

EVENING KILLER DUN

Hook: 12 fine wired up eyed, long shank if available
Silk: olive waxed
Body: pale grey hare's mask
Rib: yellow thread for the Large Green Dun or brown for the Autumn Dun
Tail: pale grey cock hackle
Wing: slips off a hen pheasant's primary quills split and advanced
Hackle: pale olive cock

With this pattern we need to achieve the illusion of size therefore I suggest that one should perhaps use a longer hackle than usual, as with the Baigent's flies we discussed earlier in the book. If you feel that you can handle it then tie it on a size 10 hook bearing in mind the dangers of line twist and need for thicker tippets. If you fish into the darkness expect hard aggressive takes when utilising this pattern and, as the Boy scouts say, be prepared.

The Autumn Dun eventually transposes into the Great Red Spinner and I would draw your attention to how this fly helped me to secure some decent trout mentioned in previous discussion regarding the River Wenning. When it is around the beck this spinner is popular with the fish.

The Large Green Dun becomes plainly the Large Green Spinner and again is well-liked with the trout when on the water, although falls of this insect can be small affairs.

Chapter 24

August often brings with it the so-called dog days when rivers dry up and fish become fickle. On the northern spate streams, both salmon and trout fishers pray to their respective gods for the greatly needed rain. Without it the migratory fish runs almost cease to come into the river system and the native brown trout are largely absent within the daylight hours. Heat reigns supreme and a feeling of lethargy greets any angler willing enough to visit the dried up beck.

One fly that can sometimes, like the BWO, seem to endure the hotter conditions is the Large Spurwing (Centroptilum pennulatum).

Its peculiar and virtually exclusive habit of sitting on rocks etc with its wings spaced out like a butterfly is rather captivating. Perhaps this is some entomological thermostatic mechanism which it uses to regulate heat exchange in the same way that butterflies do when they open and close their wings in the hot sunshine. I cannot of course be sure about this and would welcome the opinion of any knowledgeable entomologist on the issue. This habit and its smoky grey wing colouration help us to recognise it.

Who knows in another few millions years this insect might evolve into a butterfly or vice versa. Such is the great diversity of the riverbank that one can never be quite certain about how things will actually turn out. For example, some of the fossil deposits now established around locations like the River Hodder show that the entire area was once under shallow sea. Rocks imbedded with ancient crinoids older than the dinosaurs, which were once salt water plants, are now to be found in the inland becks of that and many other wild streams. Yes, Mother Nature sure does it in style when she wants to redecorate her planet.

Some excellent hatches of the Large Spurwing used to transpire on the River Lune but recently I have not noticed them in such good quantities. I hope that they reoccur and that this is just a temporary blip. Various species of insect do though increase and decrease as prevailing conditions dictate. And some are more susceptible to ecological damage, done by man in his eternally destructive quest to manipulate the planet, than others.

My greatest memories of fishing hatches of this charming insect are of shallow fast runs in warmer weather. I never recall seeing that many Large Spurwings when the days were cool. It must be a delicious insect as well for trout can become rather selective about it and ignore other species when it decides to come down in good numbers.

If you are fortunate enough to be around when the Large Spurwing is active try this dressing.

LARGE SPURWING

Hook: 16 fine wired up eyed
Silk: olive waxed
Body: pale grey hare's mask
Rib: pale yellow thread
Tail: blue dun cock hackle
Wing: slips off a coot primary quill split well and advanced
Hackle: blue dun cock

Although the female is a little paler than the male, one needn't be too pernickety about this and the same pattern will usually suffice for both sexes. Just make sure you tie those wings with a definitive split to match the natural and give the trout the correct message. And if you cannot get coot for the wing then don't worry for starling will do just as well.

As with most of my own patterns flexibility is an option. The innovative fly dresser must advance his/her own creative ideas and not follow the crowd. Learning the ropes with fly dressing will of course require some type of learnt discipline. However, as soon as the novice has gained enough proficiency I would suggest that imaginative creation of new patterns for personal benefit to be the best way forward.

When we fashion our own original dressings based only on what is seen on the water it helps us immensely. Alternatively the more restricted fly fisherman who is simply a slave to manufacturers' shop patterns, or the dressings designed by others that he just follows instructions for without question, can only trust what he is told third-hand.

One's own novel ideas, set into materialisation with easily – gained scraps of fur and feather, instinctively encourage confidence in the fly and this in turn is passed on to the fish. Positive action can only lead to more of the same in the end. You may understandably enquire 'Yes but what of the patterns given in this particular book – how can I trust them?' Well to be quite candid you cannot ever trust anyone else's patterns until you have taken them to the water, tied them on your line, cast them into the stream and caught a fish on them. That is the only true way to really ensure that they do what they, or the dresser, claims they will do.

In my own defence I will say that the dressings I have given herein are ones that I have used successfully over many years on the becks and I have no hidden motivation to foster them on anyone else. My enduring passion for the noble, wild-country art is the driving force behind these dressings – nothing more.

I include them in good faith merely as prime examples of how artificials should look in order to get you that awkward old spate stream riser. Furthermore, if you inadvertently happen to bump into me on the river and tell me that one of my dressings has performed better with say an olive rather than a blue dun hackle then I will be extremely interested in your new discovery.

We can all learn from each other and that is the way it should be. Anyone who tries to tell you that they have all the answers is a liar or a fool or both!

In the evenings one must also carry a selection of different sized sedge imitations in the fly box for the hot weather is the traditional time to float such an artificial across the path on a hungry trout. Now to be quite frank, fishing sedge artificials can be a hit and miss affair. Some evenings will see the fish pay no attention to these flies whatsoever; though on erstwhile occasions the flies will be savaged with enormous hostility.

I sense that prevailing weather conditions have a certain influence on such erratic trout behaviour. For instance, times when the fish are being rather finicky and just nosing sedges rather than taking them properly can indicate a falling glass. I am convinced that they really do feel the changes in climatic conditions much more than we ever give them credit for.

This seemingly odd theory has been proven many times for me personally. Subsequent to being faced with a frustrating day of disobliging fish the weather has thereafter indeed soured. Alternatively, pleasant evenings that are settled with the chaffinches singing harmoniously in the overhanging alders can be more productive. Then we see much enhanced sport as the fish are apparently not so agitated.

I mention climatic conditions because such natural things do I believe play a large part in fish behaviour. Grayling too are very susceptible to change and the finicky way they can behave when the weather is becoming unsettled is at times most frustrating.

Climate has of course been changing for eons and certainly long before man came on the scene. Whilst unnecessary water pollution occurs and areas of local countryside are being smashed to pieces via land hungry council-approved business developments etc, many point-scoring MP's have now apparently decided in their wisdom that we all need to do something positive for the environment by combating so-called man-made 'Global Warming'.

However, strong indications are reverberating worldwide that certain government-funded scientists are creating sensationalist theories for these funding advantages. Crafty scientists are granting the bewildered press with the usual negative sensationalism they hanker after because they know the media will of course be quite happy to publish nightmare scenarios that the world is on the brink of disaster, thanks to alleged carbon emissions created by man's actions.

Of course, numerous politicians have been very quick to take advantage of this patently dippy situation too. Unfortunately again, the professional editing process has gone out of the window and genuine analysis of factual data has been dumped in favour of unfounded alarmist hype.

Is it any coincidence that many retired well-esteemed professors and other experts, that are not now seeking extra grant funding, are usually the ones to challenge the wholesale gibberish spouted by the self-righteous climatic alarmist brigade?

All this unsubstantiated pseudo-scientific nonsense continues to be promoted by scientists, politicians and the press etc and yet at the same time our lovely wild rivers are drained and polluted by greedy industry, whilst many authorities virtually look the other way. Something is very wrong and double standards now seem to be the order of the day in society!

When August drifts into September the fish start to do something special. They know instinctively that winter is coming so they start to stack up on food. This can naturally be a bonus for the fly angler. Several species of olive that we encountered earlier in the season, like the LDO and Iron blue, now start to show up once again. Furthermore, the hatches of BWO and the Medium Olive will persist so long as the weather is not too rough.

With the onset of autumn, terrestrial insects feature quite strongly in the diet of the fish. This is when fancy patterns for grayling start to make a real impact. However, trout and sea trout are partial to these attractor flies as well at times.

One land-based or perhaps I should say tree-orientated, insect in particular can bring fish into a feeding frenzy and this is the Shield bug.

Shield bugs when fully grown are wide-bodied and flattened, insects. Adult bugs are quite fat and form a nice snack for the fish. They are quite common on river overhanging foliage around the becks during the autumn. The title Shield bug is owing to the shield-shaped appearance of the adult insects when seen from above. They feed by sucking sap from an extensive range of plants but normally cause no obvious damage to cultivated plants, even when they are plentiful.

These insects are from time to time mistaken for beetles, yet shield bugs belong to a different assembly of insects called the Hemiptera.

They lie dormant in winter as adults but prior to looking for protected places they can be seen in both late summer and autumn resting on plant foliage in the sunshine. They are nonetheless very active in early summer when they lay small bunches of eggs on the undersides of leaves. With a slight breeze they can and do get easily blown into the stream, where hungry fish take advantage. I have caught both trout and many grayling literally stuffed with different kinds of Shield bug.

It would be a mistake to visit a northern spate stream without at least a couple of chunky dressings to imitate this attractive yet ungainly looking insect.

This next undemanding dressing should be adequate for most natural Shield bug falls, yet one can of course change the colours to match whatever one encounters on particular streams.

DRY SHIELD BUG

Hook: 14 up eyed
Silk: olive waxed
Body: in two parts. At the head end bright green seal's or substitute fur dubbed on fat, at the tail end dubbed brown seal
Rib: brown thread

Hackle: short stiff green cock hackle palmered the length of the body - if preferred the hackle may be trimmed above the hook shank to give a better shape

Shield bugs are chubby creatures so do ensure that, with a dubbing needle, you pick out the body fibres to give the impression of bulk. This ruse also helps to ensure that the dressing floats well. Fish will usually take such a dressing with no messing around.

Another terrestrial that appeals to fish is the Ladybird. Many different species exist within this group and I shall not labour this issue unduly.

They are of course popular with the gardener, due to their obliging habit of feeding off both aphids and whitefly, and the fish also relish them when they fall into the water. The intense colours they display, red, orange and yellow can be achieved quite easily at the fly tying vice. The kinds we see on the streams are usually around four to six millimetres in length and mainly red although yellow ones show up from time to time. The next simple dressing with prove sufficient when ladybirds are about.

DRY LADYBIRD

Hook: 16 -20 fine wired up eyed
Silk: black waxed
Body: red seal or substitute dubbed fat
Rib: red thread
Hackle: palmered red or yellow cock – if favoured the hackle may be trimmed back above the hook shank to give a better shape

Both the Ladybird and the Shield bug may, as I stated above, have their respective hackles trimmed to form the shape of the insect. It you do this then be careful to apply enough fly floatant to stop the pattern from sinking. Personally, I would rather try the dressing with the full hackle first and only chop it down if fish were being particularly difficult to tempt. Due to the overtly thick body and palmered hackles on these two previous dressings a wing is not really required.

The Ladybird's main prey is the aphid and this little pest also forms a good part of fish diet at times.

Aphids are sap-sucking insects that can be found on numerous plants. They are one of the most universal pests to attack garden plants. I have a particular dislike for them as they dearly love to eat my mega-hot chilli plants, which I grow in summer. They are of course more frequently known as greenfly or blackly. Nevertheless, fish love to snack on these annoying pests in late summer/early autumn, ergo a few tiny dressings to match them is an obligatory part of our angling armoury. Aphids are only about one to five millimetres long so we need to keep our flies very small indeed to replicate them.

SUMMER GREENFLY

Hook: 20-24 fine wired up eyed
Silk: white waxed
Body: white tying thread
Hackle: tiny pale grizzled cock

This pattern is simplicity itself because the natural is too. Some aphids are winged whilst others are not. They are weak fliers but the breeze can carry them great distances. Just think; the greenflies that were only yesterday plaguing your prized-fruit buses may next week be hundreds of miles away helping the grayling to pack on the pounds for winter, true justice.

Balmy days can bring flying ants onto the beck and the angler who finds himself therein when flights occur is indeed a lucky soul. Literally millions of ants can tumble down onto streams during hot spells and the fish love them. Even the seemingly hopeless angling conditions posed by low water and heat can be instantly transformed if ants come down. However, many fishermen make the blunder of using patterns which are simply much too large. Ants are tiny creatures so do bear this vital point in mind. Most are only around five millimetres in body length except for the rarer queens which may reach fifteen millimetres.

This pattern will usually do the trick when ants swarm.

FLYING ANT

Hook: 18-22 fine wire, up eyed
Silk: fine black waxed
Body: black thread
Wing: small short bunch of creamy cock hackle fibres
Hackle: short black cock

Aim to create an ant-shaped body and apply a touch of fly tying varnish to give it a nice shine.

Another insect that sometimes finds itself stuck in the current of the beck is the ominous looking Devil's coach horse (Staphylinus olens). This spectacular beetle preys on caterpillars, flies, slugs and also carrion. It can give a nasty bite when threatened and draw blood too. It's quite common in hedgerows, woods and pasture. With a body length of around twenty five millimetres it forms a protein-packed mouthful if washed into the river for any hungry fish. If you spot a large black insect of these proportions struggling in the water than there's a good chance it will be a Devil's coach horse.

It's also known as the Cocktail beetle due to its habit of raising its tail in a self-protective posture. However, they are largely nocturnal so one is not as likely to see them during the daytime. It may not lend itself to light-line presentation due to its bulk yet this next pattern will suffice at times.

DRY DEVIL'S COACH HORSE

Hook: 12 long shank
Silk: black waxed
Body: dubbed black wool
Thorax: black wool
Rib: silver wire
Hackle: short black cock

In effect this dressing will appear somewhat like a lake fisherman's nymph, although it is fished dry.

I have on occasion been amazed at late season trout and the aggressive way in which the attack bees and wasps that now and then crash onto the water's surface. This usually happens on wider streams when these gawky insects get caught out wanting by a swift blast of wind, which sends them spinning into the ripple below. I also think that sudden expected cold streams of air during a hot spell may possibly cause high-flying insects to plummet earthwards on occasion.

Whatever the reason, trout are not afraid to nail wasps or bees and seem to be unaffected by their stings. If this is so then perhaps it gives more credence to some people who claim fish have little or no feeling when hooked in the mouth by an angler.

This dressing will work on stubborn fish at times that have refused other offerings put in front of them by the angler.

DRY BUMBLE

Hook: 14 - 12 fine wire, up eyed
Silk: black waxed
Body: dubbed black and yellow wool well picked out
Wing: two blue dun or creamy hackle-points
Hackle: short black cock

Dress the body quite fat to replicate the bulk of the insect. Larger hooks than stated may be utilised if you can match them to thicker leaders.

Some of the flies with slightly nastier habits also prove useful to us in autumn. Bluebottles, Houseflies, Greenbottles etc are always worth imitating at this period.

I recall one particular day on a little spate stream in mid-autumn.
The trout season had finished yet the promise of grayling was strong for the dried up golden leaves came down stream like little sailboats and fish were rising well.

The day was quite stunning, picture postcard in fact with a robin singing cheerfully in the hawthorns behind me and the warm autumn sunshine on my face. Nevertheless, something was not right for a most foul stench drifted from up the river and made me feel rather sick. The aroma of old death is something which most fishermen will encounter sooner or later on their travels.

As I meandered towards the sickening stink I noticed it was a large dead sheep which had obviously been drowned, subsequent to the last big flood on the river some two days ago. It was wedged between a large boulder and a broken oak branch on the far side of the beck, several yards away from me.

Although this was not a pleasant spectacle I also noticed several good fish rising downstream of the sheep. They were obviously interested in something and a closer look confirmed my suspicions. Dozens of frantic bluebottles were busily swarming around the carcass and some were getting caught up in the flow and washed down.

I instantly tied on a bluebottle imitation and cast out. Almost as soon as it landed a lusty grayling crashed into my fly and before long I was into battle. To cut a longer story short, within the next ten minutes several more nice silver ladies were grassed and all on the dry bluebottle.

A simple dressing for Bluebottle or Greenbottle imitation is as follows.

DRY BOTTLE FLY

Hook: 16 - 12 fine wire, up eyed
Silk: black waxed
Body: blue or green silk
Rib: Peacock herl or black ostrich herl
Wing: two blue dun hackle-points
Hackle: short black cock

Formulate the body a little on the plump side for this dressing, via running the body silk up and down the shank several times. A touch of fly tying varnish applied after the body is put on can help to secure the rib and give additional shine and durability to one's fly.

It would be quite remiss of me not to mention caterpillars that find their way into the stream, via falling off trees and shrubs above rivers. Most will be the larvae of moths as they number around two thousand five hundred different species whilst butterfly species number only about fifty six. Many wonderful butterfly species and moths too have been lost due to urban sprawl, intensive farming and lack of woodland management.

It would take a separate volume to try and recognise and give imitations for the multitude of butterfly and moth larvae that could be discovered within our streams, yet one or two general impression patterns may help to save us from an otherwise blank day on occasion. Try the following when all else fails.

DRY GREEN CATERPILLAR

Hook: 12 – 20 long shank
Silk: olive waxed
Body: green floss
Rib: Peacock herl
Hackle: short ginger cock, just a few turns will suffice

    I advocate that a series of caterpillar dressings be tied in various sizes and divergent colours to match whatever is encountered on the stream. For a fatter body use dubbed fur and pick it out with a dubbing needle. Palmered hackles are also good in such dressings at times and you can also trim them short if need be.
    Grasshopper can also figure strongly in the trout's diet in the warm months around autumn. At times they can be relatively silly creatures and a long jump that develops into a flight will frequently see them come plummeting down in the beck. Furthermore, they can leap twenty times their own body length and obtain respectable speeds of up to eight miles per hour. Due to this, grasshoppers really do come down with a hefty splash when they get their navigation wrong or when a breeze catches them out.
    Of course such a large twitching insect on the surface will bring about violent responses from any hungry fish present. Grayling too enjoy big grasshoppers when they are on the look out of a big tasty snack.

Above: A quaint old picture of the author fishing Yorkshire's exquisite River Greta.

There are literally thousands of different grasshopper species so to try an imitate them all would probably demand a fly box as big as a garden shed and the patience of a world-class chess master. In addition, the females can be considerably larger than the males so one would need to utilise two moderately substantial garden sheds. Nevertheless, one or two general patterns will usually achieve all that the angler desires when these fascinating insects are leaping around.

Try this pattern for grasshoppers.

DRY GRASSHOPPER

Hook: 12 – 14 long shank
Silk: olive waxed

Body: green, yellow, brown or grey dubbed wool or fur
Rib: gold wire
Hackle: short pale ginger cock
Legs: a few cock pheasant tail fibres tied in behind the hackle

    Another good method is to mix up the body colours given to create a mish-mash of shades which look quite attractive. The legs can also be made to appear more lifelike by tying them in as two loops, which will give the impression of the large powerful legs grasshoppers use to catapult themselves into the air. Dub the body quite thickly to make it look natural and aid with floatation. And as usual do remember that larger dressings like this one require stouter tippets.

    We have now covered the majority of insects which the fly fisher is likely to encounter on the northern spate rivers. Nevertheless, one will of course always discover miscellaneous species that occur on a given stream. In many ways this is a great part of the excitement of visiting a new beck, one never quite knows what insects will be there capturing the attention of the fish.

    The dressings I have given throughout this book will however serve for most practical purposes and ensure, if tied in various sizes, that the dry fly angler has the right tools for the job. It for some reason you cannot identify a certain insect, don't worry too much. Just set to work trying to find the most likely candidate in you fly box to match it. If, after all your hard efforts, the trout still refuses the dressings which you have good faith in then don't despair – just amble off up the beck and search out another riser. The awkward fish will probably still be in the same spot later on, so you can always give him another try then.

    'Going with the flow' is of course a contemporary phrase which, when applies to this ancient rustic art, fits in so very well.

Above: the author in action with a dry fly rod on the Lune

If you are trying too hard then indeed you are trying too hard and need to rethink your current riverside strategy. Let the fish dictate your movements and let them put you in the right place with the correct dressing. They and their kind have been around a lot longer than us and will most likely outlast us in millions of years to come. Watch, listen, think, feel and gain greater knowledge. Allow the ancient hidden magic of the stream to speak intimately to you.

Never ever force yourself on the aquatic inhabitants of the beck for if you do they will always have the last laugh.

Chapter 25

Trout and grayling are not the only residents found in the rough streams of the north and they are not the only species that will take a fly.

Two other types of fish will on occasion be encountered and although some anglers will despise their attentions, the chub and the dace deserve a mention if nothing else out of all fairness.

The existing UK chub record, so I'm informed, stands at almost nine pounds so as one can see they can attain very good sizes. Fish of that weight would be quite something on light fly gear and on warm summer days they can be caught on some of the stretches of the Ribble, Lune, Wyre and Hodder etc with dry fly.

Chub like to potter around in groups of four to say seven fish under overhanging trees during summer. They lie waiting, in an exceedingly unperturbed fashion, under the shade of oaks, willows and alders etc for hapless insects to drop onto the surface. There's never any rush about the way they go about their business and deep pools are often preferred by them.

Always make sure you have a pair of Polaroids with you too for its quite fascinating to watch these fish as they take flies just under the surface, even in the deeper stretches. Chub can frequently follow a natural or indeed one's artificial for several yards downstream before either taking it with a sudden rush or turning their backs on it in apparent disgust.

They are at times incredibly suspicious and the angler must treat them with all due respect if he wants to catch them. They are also highly curious and on numerous occasions when I have been about to net a trout or grayling, I have suddenly noticed chub swimming over to watch the action. They are indeed very nosey and will really queue up to follow a hooked fish to the net, just to see what's going on. I have noticed the same bizarre behaviour when I have caught salmon and sea trout and it's quite entertaining to see these fish driven to such inquisitiveness.

I think that their actions may be based on semi-aggressive drives though and that they are at these times perhaps planning to attack the hooked fish as it struggles to the net. So far no chub has ever actually attacked my quarry but it has been touch and go. It can indeed be quite a shock to see large chub rush at your net as you are about to land a game fish.

They will savage the lures of salmon anglers too at times so doubtless they can be hostile if the mood takes them.

Their intrinsic yet somewhat amusing curiosity extends to the flies that pass their watery lair. They can frequently be seen to swirl and nose either one's dressing or a real olive, cheeky enough to invade their territory. However, the clumsy angler's one careless footstep will send a whole shoal rushing madly out of the pool. Yes, they are extremely easily to spook.

Their finicky conduct holds true more with large flies than smaller ones. The tiny olives and terrestrials are usually taken without any undue fuss into their huge mouths, yet let a big wildly fluttering sedge or dun rove into the chub's aquatic domain and it's a different matter altogether. The way that a growling terrier instantly reacts in expectancy to a cat that inadvertently strolls into its garden is a suitable comparison herein of how chub respond to bigger flies. Nevertheless, when a chub does take a large fly it usually does so positively and gets itself hooked well. And yes, as other writer's have claimed they do on occasion like a little bit of red in the dressings.

I do not though subscribe to just throwing any old gigantic attractor patterns at chub willy-nilly. Perhaps the sort of slipshod belief that encourages that type of disregard for the species is based largely on ignorance of their actual feeding habits. Furthermore, it may have orientated from a lackadaisical freshwater angling attitude to the real nature of fly fishing for such fish. Chucking any old bushy fly at chub and hoping for the best may appeal to some, yet I personally believe we can do much better than this.

Their feeding habits on the surface must be analysed closely just like any other fish if one is to tempt them. If a large chub has taken up residence in a flow and can clearly be seen regularly taking a steady trickle of Pale Watery Duns, then that is the fly of course to replicate. Why give this feeding fish anything else if that's what he wants, there and then?

Naturally, there will be occasions when a solitary chub, or indeed a whole shoal of chub, are not taking any specific fly. Then is the time to experiment with various size dressings. Moreover, they do seem to react well to extremes. By this latter comment I mean that if say one has tried a large bushy fly without success then a switch to a tiny pattern may produce good results. By the same token, if one has been fruitlessly employing a very small fly then the change to an outsized dressing can do the trick. They are exceedingly chary and yet they are very concerned with just about any possible food item that comes skulking past their position. Remember, they do not get so big by ignoring nutritional items and have to work hard to keep their weight up.

Apart from their size I believe that one of the greatest attractions about catching chub on dry fly is their questioning nature. One can never quite know what they will make of the next fly that we drift painstaking past their noses. Will they take it, drown it, swirl hastily around if or just move away from it ever so gently in the stream? One can never be sure and that is their great charm.

I have personally taken nice chub in the rivers Lune, Wyre etc yet the largest I have caught have been from the Hodder. Sadly I never keep a proper record of weights but I firmly believe some must have been close to the six pound mark.

Pools that attract cattle down to the water to drink also seem to draw in chub. This may be due to the smell which can bring in scores of flies, especially terrestrial-based ones. I have to say though that chub are not fussy about being upstream or down stream and can tolerate all manner of waters. In fact one can discover them from the mountainous and highly-oxygenated grayling streams to the tidal reaches of our northern rivers.

The last chub I spotted rising where in a muddy tidal stretch of the River Alt, which runs through Formby near to Liverpool. They are such an adaptable species that you have just got to admire their resilience.

Hot humid summer days when all is still are excellent times to stealthily take on the chub with dry fly. You will find them lazily relaxing under old overhanging boughs in the stream; they certainly are fond of a bit of shade too. The secret is to move extremely slowly and keep low. If you crash into the water and wade towards them ineptly then say farewell to your chub, for they will simply shoot off like a flock of terrified birds.

If you are fortunate you will spot them in their idyllic resting positions. Never rush them and vigilantly study what they are rising to. If they are not moving to flies then just watch carefully for a wee while. Before long one or two members will probably take a snap at something flittering past their sight line and give you the clue required to replicate the food stuff present.

Even on fairly heavily peat-stained waters where they are not visible they usually make their presence known. Many an inexperienced angler may be forgiven for thinking that the regular huge swells and crashes under trees were salmon when in fact it was a shoal of portly chub.

They are a bit of a mystery at times too. They can appear in a stretch and then disappear like ghosts for months at a time from usual positions that they previously guarded so well. Some summers will see chub strongly in evidence whilst in other seasons they are totally absent. Perhaps they are more nomadic than we give them credit for. Alternatively, perhaps they just slope up to other pools to search out richer pickings. Personally, I think this odd behaviour may be once again due to their great intrinsic curiosity.

Although a huge chub turning up unexpectedly to the fly may disillusion, or even infuriate, some of the more traditionalist types of fly anglers this species should never be shunned.

The old curious chub is a lovely robust fish that can turn an otherwise uninspiring day into a time to remember for the open-minded fly fisher, who wants to enjoy whatever sport is available on that particular day.

The dace is another species which can crop up in some of the becks on occasion. Again, summer is a great time to discover this species and although they are not as large as chub they can provide exhilarating sport on the right day.

A twelve ounce dace is a big one and a one pounder is a real monster yet they rise freely to fly and pack into good-sized shoals to feed. A large dace may easily be mistaken for a small chub yet the anal fin on dace is concave while a chub's is convex. The dace also has a smaller mouth, which I believe may be a logical reason why hefty flies with bushy hackles are harder for it to take. Chub are altogether heavier fish in appearance, unlike the dace which is quite graceful.

The River Ribble in particular holds countless dace shoals in the lower stretches around Ribchester and they take tiny flies with great haste. They are however predominantly absent as one gets upstream into the more mountainous tributaries. Larger patterns do not seem to have quite as positive effect on dace as small ones so do fish extremely fine and light. Strikes need to be undertaken with lightening speed to secure fish and any of the usual trout patterns will easily suffice for this species.

As usual watch vigilantly for signs of what the fish are feeding on then match it as well as you possibly can. If you have never fished dry fly for the dace you will most likely be surprised at how fast they hit your dressings.

One thing's for sure though, after an invigorating day with dace you will have sharpened your instincts and have little trouble connecting with other species when they take the fly.

I mention the two previous spate stream species out of common interest to the angler.

The mainstay of our fishing will of course be aligned around the brown trout and the grayling, which rule the various streams I have mentioned throughout this book.

Above: the real star of any dry fly fishing show and a fitting conclusion to this book. Olives like this one make up a large part of the diet of our quarry.

Some streams are well filled with both these game species, whilst grayling are absent from others. By the same token salmon and sea trout are not able to surmount many obstacles such as huge waterfalls in certain areas leading to their own absence therein. None of these things matter, for whatever species is encountered one thing alone counts more than the rest. The chance to experience the magnificent northern spate rivers is there for anyone who is drawn to such wild bleak places.

The seasonal love affair with these wonderful old waterways only increases each year for the resilient souls who make the effort to visit them.

It is my sincere wish that the hard-gleaned material passed on throughout this book will inspire more individuals to allow their own angling passions to be fulfilled.

Let the ancient meandering stream show you the way – it will if you only care to listen!

Author links:

http://patregan.jimdo.com

http://www.patregan.allalla.com

http://pat-regan.blogspot.co.uk

https://www.facebook.com/reganclan

http://dryflyfisher.yolasite.com

Fly fishing on wild becks

Secrets of the hidden stream

By

Pat Regan, Southport.

One last thing…

When you turn the page, Kindle will give you the opportunity to rate this book and share your thoughts on Facebook, Google and Twitter. If you believe the book is worth sharing, would you take a few seconds to let your friends know about it? If they find it enjoyable they will be grateful, as will I.

All the Best,

Pat Regan

Printed in Great Britain
by Amazon.co.uk, Ltd.,
Marston Gate.